Express Web Application Development

Learn how to develop web applications with the Express framework from scratch

Hage Yaapa

BIRMINGHAM - MUMBAI

Express Web Application Development

First published: June 2013

Production Reference: 1190613

Published by Packt Publishing Ltd.
Livery Place
35 Livery Street
Birmingham B3 2PB, UK.

ISBN 978-1-84969-654-8

www.packtpub.com

Cover Image by Jarek Blaminsky (milak6@wp.pl)

Credits

Author
Hage Yaapa

Reviewers
Jim Alateras
Johan Borestad
Sinisa Vrhovac

Acquisition Editor
Erol Staveley

Lead Technical Editor
Dayan Hyames

Technical Editor
Dominic Pereira

Project Coordinator
Shiksha Chaturvedi

Proofreader
Chris Smith

Indexer
Monica Ajmera Mehta

Graphics
Hage Yaapa

Production Coordinator
Aditi Gajjar

Cover Work
Aditi Gajjar

About the Author

Hage Yaapa is a contributing developer of Express and the head of Web and Node.js development at Sourcebits.

He joined one of the best medical schools in India, JIPMER, to become a doctor, but dropped out to pursue his burning passion for computers and the Internet. He has been creating websites and apps since 1999 using a very wide array of web technologies. He is a self-taught programmer and everything he knows about technology, he learned on his own from the Internet and books.

Yaapa blogs about Node.js, Express, and other web technologies on his website `www.hacksparrow.com`, as Captain Hack Sparrow.

This will sound crazy, but I would like to first thank Khaled Mardam-Bey, the creator of mIRC—the IRC software, which started everything for me. I learned many of the important things I know about computers and the Internet on IRC channels during the transitioning of the century. The first programming language I learned was mIRC Script, which helped me pick up JavaScript and other programming languages rather easily.

Next, I would like to thank T. J. Holowaychuk for creating Express and the unbelievable number of impressive Node.js packages he has created.

Then, I would like to thank Ryan Dahl for creating Node.js, and Isaac Schlueter for carrying it forward.

I would also like to thank Brendan Eich for creating JavaScript, for there would have been no Node.js or Express, if there were no JavaScript.

Last but not the least, I would like to thank my loving wife Kenyum for putting up with me while I wrote this book.

About the Reviewers

Jim Alateras is an independent consultant specializing in open source and emerging technologies. He has a degree in Electrical/Electronic Engineering and has been working in the software development space for more than 25 years. Jim has participated in several open source projects, presented at open source conferences, and has written several articles and contributed to books. Currently, he is working on developing large-scale, real-time applications using Node.js and the amazing number of great modules and frameworks.

Johan Borestad is a senior web developer, living together with his fiancée Sophia in Stockholm, Sweden. He's a former CTO for `Videofy.me` and has been working with several startup companies (`Redbet.com`, `Reco.se`) in the past from where he has collected invaluable experience, both from backend and frontend. His main skills lie within Test Driven Development and scalable cross-browser web applications. In his daily work he prefers to work with Ruby and JavaScript.

Today he's working at Klarna—one of Sweden's most promising startup companies—building the future e-commerce experience with *Klarna Checkout*.

I'd like to thank my fiancée Sophia and my soon-to-be-born daughter Lilly for all the joy in life you give me. Without you, the passion for my work wouldn't mean a thing.

Sinisa Vrhovac is a web developer and all-round Internet technology geek living and working in Banja Luka with his family. While working with different companies, he crafted his skills in web development always trying to go one step further in order to improve user experience and comfort. Through engagement on many projects he has gained experience in many technologies and software platforms.

Sinisa enjoys time spent with family, picnics and movies. He can be contacted via LinkedIn, Facebook, or Google+.

I would like to thank my family for their support and understanding in moments when work has priorities over time to spend with family.

www.PacktPub.com

Support files, eBooks, discount offers and more

You might want to visit www.PacktPub.com for support files and downloads related to your book.

Did you know that Packt offers eBook versions of every book published, with PDF and ePub files available? You can upgrade to the eBook version at www.PacktPub.com and as a print book customer, you are entitled to a discount on the eBook copy. Get in touch with us at service@packtpub.com for more details.

At www.PacktPub.com, you can also read a collection of free technical articles, sign up for a range of free newsletters and receive exclusive discounts and offers on Packt books and eBooks.

http://PacktLib.PacktPub.com

Do you need instant solutions to your IT questions? PacktLib is Packt's online digital book library. Here, you can access, read and search across Packt's entire library of books.

Why Subscribe?

- Fully searchable across every book published by Packt
- Copy and paste, print and bookmark content
- On demand and accessible via web browser

Free Access for Packt account holders

If you have an account with Packt at www.PacktPub.com, you can use this to access PacktLib today and view nine entirely free books. Simply use your login credentials for immediate access.

Table of Contents

Preface

This book is about Express, the popular web framework used by thousands of Node.js developers around the world. It specifically covers the third major version of the framework, commonly referred to as Express 3.

Express has matured considerably since it was first released exactly four years ago. Today it is recognized as one of the best web frameworks for Node.js. Every day new developers from varied backgrounds and experience come to Express for developing their web apps. With its ever-growing popularity, it is about time we had a book on Express.

I wrote a tutorial on Express some time ago that became quite popular online, particularly with those new to Node.js and Express. Ever since, I had a dream of writing a book on Express, which would make no assumptions about the reader's prior experience and knowledge, and still be full of technical details wherever required. The book you are holding in your hands is that dream realized—a book on Express that is both beginner-friendly and technically deep at the same time.

This book covers everything a developer requires to get into serious web development using Express.

What this book covers

Chapter 1, What is Express?, is a beginner-friendly but technically solid introduction to Express and relevant topics for a strong base right at the start.

Chapter 2, Your First Express App, is a practical introduction to building an Express app covering the basics that form the basis of every Express app.

Chapter 3, Understanding Express Routes, explains routes in Express in great detail.

Chapter 4, Response From the Server, covers the various ways an Express app can respond to a request.

Chapter 5, The Jade Templating Language, covers the Jade syntax and its programming capabilities.

Chapter 6, The Stylus CSS Preprocessor, covers the Stylus syntax and its programming capabilities.

Chapter 7, Forms, Cookies, and Sessions, covers how to handle forms, and create cookies and sessions.

Chapter 8, Express in Production, covers important areas to make Express apps production-ready.

What you need for this book

Familiarity with JavaScript, the command line, and interest in the subject are all you need to get the most out of the book. Any new and relevant topics are introduced and explained in an easy-to-understand manner.

Who this book is for

This book is for anyone interested in knowing more about Express—either for developing web applications or just for technical knowledge in general. It is friendly enough for beginners to get started with, at the same time detailed enough to make an excellent refresher for those already familiar with Express who want to know more about it.

Conventions

In this book, you will find a number of styles of text that distinguish between different kinds of information. Here are some examples of these styles, and an explanation of their meaning.

Code words in text, database table names, folder names, filenames, file extensions, pathnames, dummy URLs, user input, and Twitter handles are shown as follows: "The `router` middleware is responsible for handling the requests to the app."

A block of code is set as follows:

```
app.get('/', function(req, res) {
  res.json({message: 'welcome'});
});
```

When we wish to draw your attention to a particular part of a code block, the relevant lines or items are set in bold:

```
var not_found = function(req, res) {
  res.status(404);
  res.render('404', {title: 'Not Found'});
};
```

Any command-line input or output is written as follows:

```
$ sudo npm install express -g
```

New terms and **important words** are shown in bold. Words that you see on the screen, in menus or dialog boxes for example, appear in the text like this: "The server will respond with the appropriate data type based on the **Accept** header."

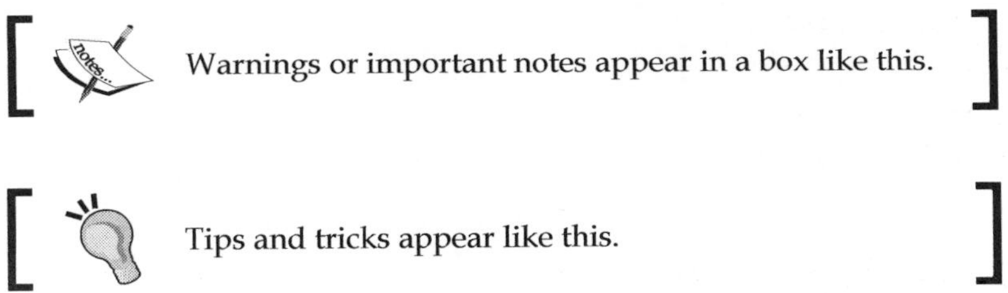

Warnings or important notes appear in a box like this.

Tips and tricks appear like this.

Reader feedback

Feedback from our readers is always welcome. Let us know what you think about this book—what you liked or may have disliked. Reader feedback is important for us to develop titles that you really get the most out of.

To send us general feedback, simply send an e-mail to `feedback@packtpub.com`, and mention the book title via the subject of your message.

If there is a topic that you have expertise in and you are interested in either writing or contributing to a book, see our author guide on `www.packtpub.com/authors`.

Downloading the example code

You can download the example code fi les for all Packt books you have purchased from your account at `http://www.packtpub.com`. If you purchased this book elsewhere, you can visit `http://www.packtpub.com/support` and register to have the fi les e-mailed directly to you.

Customer support

Now that you are the proud owner of a Packt book, we have a number of things to help you to get the most from your purchase.

Errata

Although we have taken every care to ensure the accuracy of our content, mistakes do happen. If you find a mistake in one of our books—maybe a mistake in the text or the code—we would be grateful if you would report this to us. By doing so, you can save other readers from frustration and help us improve subsequent versions of this book. If you find any errata, please report them by visiting `http://www.packtpub.com/submit-errata`, selecting your book, clicking on the **errata submission form** link, and entering the details of your errata. Once your errata are verified, your submission will be accepted and the errata will be uploaded on our website, or added to any list of existing errata, under the Errata section of that title. Any existing errata can be viewed by selecting your title from `http://www.packtpub.com/support`.

Piracy

Piracy of copyright material on the Internet is an ongoing problem across all media. At Packt, we take the protection of our copyright and licenses very seriously. If you come across any illegal copies of our works, in any form, on the Internet, please provide us with the location address or website name immediately so that we can pursue a remedy.

Please contact us at `copyright@packtpub.com` with a link to the suspected pirated material.

We appreciate your help in protecting our authors, and our ability to bring you valuable content.

Questions

You can contact us at `questions@packtpub.com` if you are having a problem with any aspect of the book, and we will do our best to address it.

1
What is Express?

This chapter is a beginner-friendly introduction to Express. Along with the basics, you will learn about the core concepts and components that make up an Express app. While we won't be doing a lot of coding in this time, the chapter will orient and condition you to Express, which will prepare you for the upcoming chapters.

Do not skip this chapter, the material covered here provide the map and compass to your journey of learning Express.

What is Express?

Express is a minimal yet flexible and powerful web development framework for the **Node.js** (Node) platform.

What do we mean by minimal yet flexible and powerful?

Express is minimal because it does not come loaded with all sorts of functionality, which makes it a bloat-free framework. Out of the box, it supports only the very basic features of a web framework. Even the supported features are not all enabled by default, you have the option to pick and use, according to your needs.

The flexibility in Express comes from the use of middlewares and Node modules. Express middlewares and Node modules are pluggable JavaScript components, which make Express apps very modular, flexible, and extensible.

Express is a powerful framework because it gives you complete access to the core Node APIs. Anything you can do with Node, you can do it with Express too.

Express can be used to create very simple to very complex web apps. It provides you all the tools required to create the most complex of apps, but does not force you to use them when you don't need them.

Hearing someone tell you that Express is a minimal, flexible, and powerful web development framework doesn't really help much in understanding it, does it?. Many other frameworks probably claim the same thing. Let's find out what is actually special about Express.

The story of Express

There is an interesting story behind the origin of Express. You will understand Express better if you know the story, so let me share the story of how Express came into being.

Sometime in February 2009, Ryan Dahl had an epiphany about combining JavaScript and Google's V8 engine to create a new system-level programming platform. He christened the platform as Node.js (Node), and released v0.0.1 in the same month.

Node was very well received by the web development community, and it started to grow very rapidly in popularity.

Apart from being a general-purpose software development platform, Node provided a web server API (Application Programming Interface), using which developers could create web apps using JavaScript as the backend programming language.

However, there was a problem with Node's web server API: It was a little too low level, and you had to write and re-write many of the web server functions in your web apps. Modularity and extensibility became a problem for any project that was even moderately big.

Within five months of Node's release, in June 2009, T.J. Holowaychuk, released an open source project named **Express** to make web development a little easier in Node.

Express was inspired by Ruby's **Sinatra** and built on top of Node's web server API. It was a little crude, but provided some of the niceties—such as a routing system, session and cookie support, MIME helpers, RESTful interface, HAML-based views, and so on—one might expect from a web development framework.

However, Express v0.0.1 was very different from what Express 3 is today. Perhaps, the only thing common in between them is the name "Express".

In June 2010, Sencha, under its Sencha Labs, started an open source project named **Connect**, to solve the modularity and extensibility issue in the Node web server API. The project was inspired by Ruby's **Rack** web server interface. Tim Caswell, a Sencha employee, and T.J. Holowaychuk, were roped in to lead the project.

Like Express, Connect was also built on top of Node's web server API, and came with a middleware system, which allowed small re-usable programs to be plugged onto it to handle HTTP-specific functionalities.

Connect middlewares took care of many of the commonly required functionalities in web apps for Node. On top of that, anyone could write their own middleware for their apps. Connect considerably improved the modularity and extensibility of the Node web server API.

By now, there were two different web development frameworks for Node: Express and Connect—one was inspired by Sinatra, and the other by Rack. This caused a bit of confusion in the Node community, especially with Holowaychuk working on both of them.

But as luck would have it, it became obvious that Express and Connect were actually complementary frameworks. So, in July 2010, Holowaychuk decided to re-architect Express to run on top of Connect, effectively merging Connect with Express to create a new incarnation of Express in v1.0.0.

With Express v1.0.0, there was no more confusion about which web development framework to choose in Node. Express was Connect with additional functionalities built on top of it. To this day it remains the same—Express continues to use the Connect middleware, and any change in Connect is invariably reflected in Express.

So, that is the story of how Express came into being and how Connect is related to it.

As an Express developer, you might rarely deal with Connect directly, but you will be using a lot of middlewares in your projects. Middlewares in Express are referred to as Express middlewares and not Connect middlewares, although technically they are Connect middlewares. You will learn more about middlewares in upcoming sections in this and the next chapter.

Installing Express

Installing Express is pretty straightforward, especially if you have Node installed already. Even if you don't have Node installed, you need not worry, because I will show you how to install Express from scratch, and that includes installing Node.

If you are on a Windows or Mac machine, installing Node is very easy—just download the respective installer from `http://nodejs.org/download/`. On Linux machines, the installation process is a little more elaborate. I will show you how to install Node on an Ubuntu machine.

For a relatively easier and cleaner installation of Node, you can use **Node Version Manager (nvm)**. Besides installing Node, it will help you flexibly switch to any version of Node right on your machine. Read more about nvm at `https://github.com/creationix/nvm`.

Before we go about installing Node, let's make sure we have the required dependencies on the system by executing the following command:

```
$ sudo apt-get -y install build-essential g++ libssl-devpkg-config
```

With that, we are ready to start installing Node. Let's get the source code from the Node download page located at `http://nodejs.org/download/`. At the time of writing, the source code was located at `http://nodejs.org/dist/v0.10.7/node-v0.10.7.tar.gz`. Let's download the source code archive to the `/tmp` directory and install Node from there:

```
$ cd /tmp
$ wget http://nodejs.org/dist/v0.10.7/node-v0.10.7.tar.gz
$ tar zxvf node-v0.10.7.tar.gz
$ cd node-v0.10.7
$ ./configure
$ make
$ sudo make install
```

If everything went fine, you have Node installed on your system now. Let's confirm it with a quick Node version check command:

```
$ node -v
> v0.10.7
```

Congratulations! Let's go install Express now.

As I mentioned earlier, installing Express is very straightforward once you have Node installed on your system.

Express is a Node module, and like any other Node module, it is installed using the **Node Package Manager (npm)**, which comes installed with Node by default. You will learn more about npm and Node modules in a later section.

Node modules come in two variants: **local** and **global**. Local modules are meant to be used in a specific project, and are available only for that particular project, while global modules are installed system-wide, and are almost always available as a command-line tool.

Express is meant to be installed as a global module, so that we can use its `express` command-line tool to generate Express app skeletons quickly.

> Express is the web development framework. `express` is the command-line tool to create Express app skeletons.

We specify the `-g` option in the `npm install` command to install Node modules as global modules. Here is the command to install Express:

```
$ sudo npm install express -g
```

That command will install the latest stable version of Express. In case, you want to install a specific version of Express, you can specify the version using the `@` parameter in the module name. Here is an example of installing an older version of Express:

```
$ sudo npm install express@3.0.5 -g
```

After the installation process is complete, confirm you are able to execute the `express` command, with a version check:

```
$ express -V
> 3.2.6
```

Congrats! Your system is ready for Express development now.

The stuff that makes up Express

A good thing about Express is that there are only three core components to it, which makes it relatively easy to know a lot about Express, if not master it entirely. In this section, I will give a brief introduction about each of the core Express components, so that you are not left disoriented when you come across them in the coming chapters.

The application object

The application object is an instance of Express, conventionally represented by the variable named `app`. This is the main object of your Express app and the bulk of the functionality is built on it.

This is how you create an instance of the Express module:

```
var express = require('express');
var app = new express();
```

The following is a brief description of all the properties and methods available on the application object:

Property/Method	Description
`app.set(name, value)`	Sets app-specific properties
`app.get(name)`	Retrieves value set by `app.set()`
`app.enable(name)`	Enables a setting in the app
`app.disable(name)`	Disables a setting in the app
`app.enabled(name)`	Checks if a setting is enabled
`app.disabled(name)`	Checks if a setting is disabled
`app.configure([env], callback)`	Sets app settings conditionally based on the development environment
`app.use([path], function)`	Loads a middleware in the app
`app.engine(ext, callback)`	Registers a template engine for the app
`app.param([name], callback)`	Adds logic to route parameters
`app.VERB(path, [callback...], callback)`	Defines routes and handlers based on HTTP verbs
`app.all(path, [callback...], callback)`	Defines routes and handlers for all HTTP verbs
`app.locals`	The object to store variables accessible from any view
`app.render(view, [options], callback)`	Renders view from the app
`app.routes`	A list of routes defined in the app
`app.listen()`	Binds and listen for connections

The request object

The HTTP request object is created when a client makes a request to the Express app. The object is conventionally represented by a variable named `req`, which contains a number of properties and methods related to the current request.

The following table lists all the properties and methods of the `req` object and provides a brief description of them:

Property/Method	Description
`req.params`	Holds the values of named routes parameters
`req.params(name)`	Returns the value of a parameter from named routes or `GET` params or `POST` params
`req.query`	Holds the values of a `GET` form submission
`req.body`	Holds the values of a `POST` form submission
`req.files`	Holds the files uploaded via a form
`req.route`	Provides details about the current matched route
`req.cookies`	Cookie values
`req.signedCookies`	Signed cookie values
`req.get(header)`	Gets the request HTTP header
`req.accepts(types)`	Checks if the client accepts the media types
`req.accepted`	A list of accepted media types by the client
`req.is(type)`	Checks if the incoming request is of the particular media type
`req.ip`	The IP address of the client
`req.ips`	The IP address of the client, along with that of the proxies it is connected through
`req.path`	The request path
`req.host`	Hostname from the HTTP header
`req.fresh`	Checks if the request is still fresh
`req.stale`	Checks if the request is stale
`req.xhr`	Checks if the request came via an AJAX request
`req.protocol`	The protocol used for making the request
`req.secure`	Checks if it is a secure connection
`req.subdomains`	Subdomains of the host domain name
`req.url`	The request path, along with any query parameters
`req.originalUrl`	Used as a backup for `req.url`
`req.acceptedLanguages`	A list of accepted languages by the client

Property/Method	Description
`req.acceptsLanguage(langauge)`	Checks if the client accepts the language
`req.acceptedCharsets`	A list of accepted charsets by the client
`req.acceptsCharsets(charset)`	Checks if the client accepts the charset

The response object

The response object is created along with the request object, and is conventionally represented by a variable named `res`. While it may sound a little strange that both of them should be created together, it is a necessity to give all the middlewares a chance to work on the request and the response object, before passing the control to the next middleware.

The following is a table of properties and methods on the response object:

Property/Method	Description
`res.status(code)`	Sets the HTTP response code
`res.set(field, [value])`	Sets response HTTP headers
`res.get(header)`	Gets the response HTTP header
`res.cookie(name, value, [options])`	Sets cookie on the client
`res.clearCookie(name, [options])`	Deletes cookie on the client
`res.redirect([status], url)`	Redirects the client to a URL, with an optional HTTP status code
`res.location`	The location value of the response HTTP header
`res.charset`	The charset value of the response HTTP header
`res.send([body|status], [body])`	Sends an HTTP response object, with an optional HTTP response code
`res.json([status|body], [body])`	Sends a JSON object for HTTP response, along with an optional HTTP response code
`res.jsonp([status|body], [body])`	Sends a JSON object for HTTP response with JSONP support, along with an optional HTTP response code
`res.type(type)`	Sets the media type HTTP response header

Property/Method	Description
`res.format(object)`	Sends a response conditionally, based on the request HTTP Accept header
`res.attachment([filename])`	Sets response HTTP header Content-Disposition to attachment
`res.sendfile(path, [options], [callback]])`	Sends a file to the client
`res.download(path, [filename], [callback])`	Prompts the client to download a file
`res.links(links)`	Sets the HTTP Links header
`res.locals`	The object to store variables specific to the view rendering a request
`res.render(view, [locals], callback)`	Renders a view

Concepts used in Express

There are a few concepts you should be familiar with before you start developing in Express. It is important that you know them, because you will be able to come up with creative and effective solutions to the challenges you might face in your projects, if you are familiar with them.

These concepts will help you understand Express better, which means more power and control to you.

Asynchronous JavaScript

Many beginners in JavaScript get stumped while using Node for the first time because they are not familiar with asynchronous (async) JavaScript and callback functions (callbacks). Node and Express are built on the concept of async operations, so it is imperative that you understand the concept before you proceed any further.

> If you have used AJAX in its default state, you are already familiar with asynchronous JavaScript. On the client-side, AJAX and timer functions are the only obvious instances where you get to see JavaScript in async mode. On Node, they are all over the place.

Unlike the more common synchronous functions, asynchronous functions do not return immediately; at the same time they do not block the execution of its succeeding code. This means other tasks are not piled up waiting for the current task to be completed. However, to resume control from the async operation and to handle its result, we need to use a callback function. The callback function is passed to the async function to be executed after the async function is done with its job.

Here is an example of using a timer to illustrate how callbacks work:

```
var broadcast = function(msg, timeout, callback) {

  // initiate an async call using a timer
  setTimeout(function() {
    // the first message
    console.log(msg);
    // execute the callback function
    callback();
  }, timeout);
};

broadcast('Is there anybody out there?', 1000, function() {
  console.log('Message sent');
});
```

We passed in a callback to the `broadcast` function, which will be executed after the message is "broadcasted" after one second.

Though Node is synonymous with async operations, it still provides a sync alternative to many of its operations. However, it is recommended to stick to the async versions, else you will very likely lose the non-blocking advantage of Node.

Node modules

A Node module is a JavaScript library that can be modularly included in Node applications using the `require()` function. What the module is capable of is entirely dependent on the module—it can be simple helper functions to something more complex such as a web development framework, which is what Express is.

If you have used `npm` to install something, you have used a node module. A lot of them are installed as command-line tools, such as the `express` command. A lot more of them are installed as libraries to be used with a Node program.

> npm is a command-line tool for installing Node modules. It comes installed with Node by default. Type `npm help` at the command line to see its various options and commands.
>
> The official website of npm is located at `https://npmjs.org/`, and you can find a huge list of Node modules at `https://github.com/joyent/node/wiki/modules`.

The bulk of web server-related functionality in Express is provided by its built-in middlewares. Features not supported by Express out of the box are implemented using Node modules.

Since Express provides just the bare minimum functionality of a web server, it does not support some common but crucial functionality, such as connecting to a database, sending e-mails, and so on. In such cases, you will need to find and install the appropriate Node modules and use them to get your task done.

The fact that Express does not come baked in with opinionated modules or methods to accomplish tasks beyond handling HTTP requests is a good thing, because it keeps the framework bloat-free and gives its users the freedom of choice to use any module or method according to their specific requirements.

The Node community is very active and has developed modules for almost every requirement on a typical web project. So remember, if you are looking to do something tricky or complex, probably there is a Node module for it already, if it does not exist, probably you should create it and share it with the Node community. If you are in no mood for sharing with others, make it a private Node module and keep it to yourself.

If it makes you wonder what is the difference between a public and a private module: public modules can be published on the `npm` registry and installed by the general public, whereas private modules remain private.

As you start working with Express, you will realize that writing your own modules will greatly help in modularizing your app. So, it is essential that you learn how to write them.

There are two approaches to writing Node modules: one involves attaching properties and functions to the `exports` object, the other involves assigning JavaScript objects to the `module.exports` property of a module.

The attachment to `exports` approach is pretty straightforward, as you can see from the following example:

```
var name = exports.name = 'Packt';
var secret = 'zoltan';
```

```
exports.lower = function(input) {
  return input.toLowerCase();
};

exports.upper = function(input) {
  return input.toUpperCase();
};

exports.get_name = function() {
  return name;
}

exports.get_secret = function() {
  return secret;
}
```

Anything attached to the `exports` objects is available as a public property or method of the instance of the module. Any variable defined with the `var` keyword and not attached to the `exports` object becomes a private variable of the module. Save the preceding example code in a file named `mymod.js`, and include it in a file named `test.js` with the following code:

```
var mod = require('./mymod.js');

console.log(mod.name);
console.log(mod.lower('APPLE'));
console.log(mod.upper('mango'));
console.log(mod.get_name());
```

Execute `test.js` to see the module in action:

```
$ node test.js
Packt
apple
MANGO
Packt
```

The assignment to `module.exports` approach is straightforward too. If you were to implement the previous module using the assignment method, this is how it would look like:

```
var secret = 'zoltan';

module.exports = {
```

```
    name: 'Packt',

    lower: function(input) {
      return input.toLowerCase();
    },

    upper: function(input) {
      return input.toUpperCase();
    },

    get_name: function() {
      return this.name;
    },

    get_secret: function() {
      return secret;
    }

};
```

There is an interesting thing about the second method of writing Node modules: you can assign any valid JavaScript object to the `module.exports` property, and it becomes the module. In the following example, we assign a function to the `module.exports` property:

```
module.exports = function(word) {

  var reversed = '';

  var i = word.length - 1;
  while (i> -1) {
    var letter = word[i];
    reversed += letter;
    i--;
  }

  return reversed;
};
```

Save the preceding code in a file named `reverse.js`. You can include it in the `test.js` file and use if for reversing text:

```
var reverse  = require('./reverse.js');
console.log(reverse('hippopotamus'));
```

Execute `test.js` again to see `reverse.js` in action:

```
$ node test.js
sumatopoppih
```

Using the assignment method, you can create Node modules to be of any valid JavaScript object type.

If you ever happen to have both the attachment and assignment methods defined in the same module file, the assignment method will take precedence.

Express apps are Node modules

It might sound a little strange, but every Express app is also a Node module. You might rarely use your web app like a regular Node module and include them in other apps, but there is something which will be an indispensable part of your app—its manifest file, `package.json`.

A manifest file is a file which contains meta data about some software. The content of the file may be used by the software to customize itself.

Node modules come with a manifest file named `package.json`, which contains details, such as its name, version, dependencies, and so on about the module.

Node modules, such as Express, which come with a `package.json` file and can be installed using `npm` are formally called Node packages. However, we will use the terms modules and packages interchangeably in the book without getting too pedantic.

Here is an example of an Express app's `package.json` file:

```
{
  "name": "application-name",
  "version": "0.0.1",
  "private": true,
  "scripts": {
    "start": "node app"
  },
  "dependencies": {
    "express": "3.2.6",
    "jade": "*",
    "stylus": "*"
  }
}
```

Among the various fields, `dependencies` is what would be of your prime interest. For an interactive guide to all the possible fields in a `package.json` file, visit `http://package.json.nodejitsu.com/`.

Any time you install a Node module in the application directory, the module will get added to the dependencies list with the version you specified. Of course, you can manually make new entries or update the version numbers of existing dependencies if you want to.

You may wonder what is the point of adding the modules in the dependencies when you already are installing them using `npm`. Well, if you start using a version control system such as Git or SVN, it doesn't make sense to include the installed Node modules in the repository. However it makes sense to include the `package.json` file, because with a simple `npm install` command in the app directory, you can reinstall the dependencies in one go.

It is advisable to use all other fields of the `package.json` file, but you certainly can't do without the dependencies key, if you are serious about your app.

By convention, the main file of the Express app is named `app.js`. You can rename it to anything you want, but it is generally not recommended to do so.

Middlewares

A middleware is a JavaScript function to handle HTTP requests to an Express app. It can manipulate the request and the response objects or perform an isolated action, or terminate the request flow by sending a response to the client, or pass on the control to the next middleware.

Middlewares are loaded in an Express app using the `app.use()` method.

Following is an example of a middleware. All it does is print the IP address of the client that made the request. Although it may seem like a trivial middleware, it gives you a very good overview of how middlewares work:

```
app.use(function(req, res, next) {
  console.log('Request from: ' + req.ip);
  next();
});
```

As you can see, a middleware is just a function that accepts three parameters: `req`, `res`, and `next`. The `req` parameter is the request object, the `res` parameter is the response object, and the `next` parameter is a reference to the next middleware in line. Any middleware can end a request by sending a response back to the client using one of the response methods on the `res` object. Any middleware that does not call a response method must call the next middleware in line, else the request will be left hanging in there.

Even though our middleware in the previous example was pretty simple, in most practical cases, middlewares will be created in a more complex fashion—they could be a JavaScript object defined right in the file, or might be included as a Node module.

This is how a middleware would look like if it were defined first and then passed to the `app.use()` method:

```
// define the middleware
var forbidder = function(forbidden_day) {

  var days = ['Sunday', 'Monday', 'Tueday', 'Wednesday', 'Thursday',
'Friday', 'Saturday'];

  return function(req, res, next) {

    // get the current day
    var day = new Date().getDay();

    // check if the current day is the forbidden day
    if (days[day] === forbidden_day) {
      res.send('No visitors allowed on ' + forbidden_day + 's!');
    }
    // call the next middleware
    else {
      next();
    }
  }
};

// use the forbidder middleware
app.use(forbidder('Wednesday'));
// the router middleware goes here
app.use(app.router);
```

This middleware forbids visitors on your website on a certain day. Probably not a very useful middleware, but the intent is to show you how a middleware works.

One thing you might have noted is that we included the `forbidder` middleware before the `router` middleware. Does it make any difference? Oh yes, it does! A middleware included earlier takes precedence over those included later. So be careful about the order of inclusion.

If we were to rewrite the `forbidder` middleware as a Node module, we would need to first create the `forbidder.js` module file with the following content:

```
module.exports = function(forbidden_day) {

  var days = ['Sunday', 'Monday', 'Tueday', 'Wednesday', 'Thursday',
'Friday', 'Saturday'];

  return function(req, res, next) {

    // get the current day
    var day = new Date().getDay();

    // check if the current day is the forbidden day
    if (days[day] === forbidden_day) {
      res.send('No visitors allowed on ' + forbidden_day + 's!');
    }
    // call the next middleware
    else {
      next();
    }
  }
};
```

Then, the module would be included in the app, and an instance of the module would be created:

```
var forbidder = require('./forbidder.js');
```

And the middleware would be added to the chain:

```
app.use(forbidder('Wednesday'));
```

The majority of top-level Express functionality is implemented via its built-in middlewares. An indispensable component of Express is the `router` middleware, which is responsible for routing the HTTP requests to your Express apps to the appropriate handler functions.

Request flow

One might be tempted to think that when you make a request to your web app, there would be a corresponding JavaScript file that would be executed by Node. For example, to load the home page, there would be a file named `home.js`, for the contact page, `contact.js`, and so on.

That's not the case in an Express app. There is a single entry point for all the requests coming to the app—via `app.js`—which bootstraps the Express framework.

When an HTTP request arrives at your app, it goes through a stack of middlewares. All the middlewares in the chain have the capacity to modify the request and the response object in any form and manner, and that's how they work, as we learned in the last section.

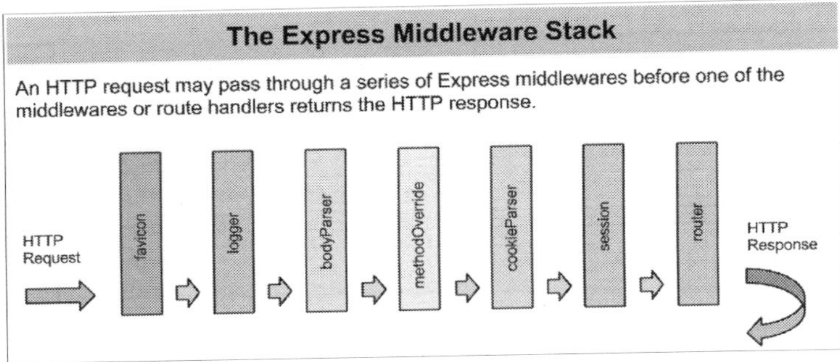

Among the middlewares, which are include in Express, the most important is the `router` middleware, which gives Express the capability to define routes and handle them.

Here is a conceptualized representation of routes and their handlers:

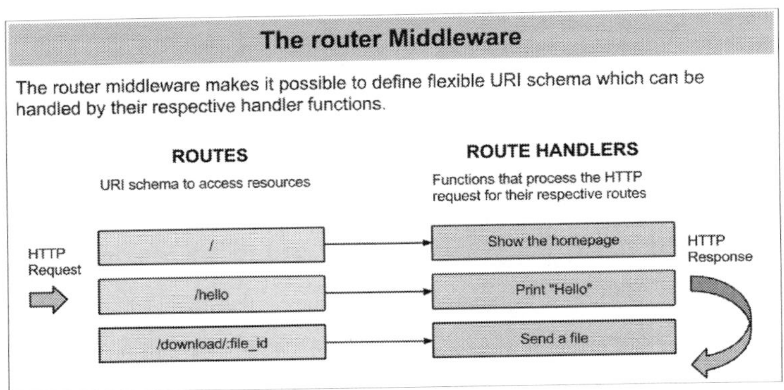

The destinations of the HTTP request URIs are defined via routes in the app. Routes are how you tell your app "for this URI, execute this piece of JavaScript code". The corresponding JavaScript function for a route is called a **route handler**. It is the responsibility of the route handler to respond to an HTTP request, or pass it on to another handler function if it does not. Route handlers may be defined in the `app.js` file or loaded as a Node module.

Here is a working example of some routes and their handlers defined right in the `app.js` file:

```
var http = require('http');
var express = require('express');
var app = express();

app.get('/', function(req, res) {
  res.send('Welcome!');
});

app.get('/hello.text', function(req, res) {
  res.send('Hola!');
});

app.get('/contact', function(req, res) {
  res.render('contact');
});

http.createServer(app).listen(3000, function(){
  console.log('Express server listening on port ' + 3000);
});
```

Defining the routes and their handlers in the `app.js` file may work fine if the number of routes is relatively few. It becomes messy if the number of routes starts growing. That's where defining the routes and their handlers in a Node module comes in handy. If we were to modularize the routes we defined earlier, here is how it would look like.

> The reason I used a strange looking route `/hello.text` is to show that route names can be anything and have no inherent meaning in Express. It is up to the route handler to give meaning and purpose to the routes.

The following is the content of the `routes.js` Node module:

```
module.exports = function(app) {

  app.get('/', function(req, res) {
```

```
    // Send a plain text response
    res.send('Welcome!');
  });

  app.get('/hello.text', function(req, res) {
    // Send a plain text response
    res.send('Hola!');
  });

  app.get('/contact', function(req, res) {
    // Render a view
    res.render('contact');
  });
};
```

The modified `app.js` file would look like the following now:

```
var http = require('http');
var express = require('express');
var app = express();
var routes = require('./routes')(app);

http.createServer(app).listen(3000, function(){
  console.log('Express server listening on port ' + 3000);
});
```

A request handler can send a response back to the client using one of the response methods in the response object. The act of sending a response effectively terminates the request flow to any other route handler.

Views are special files in an Express app, which are sent as an HTML response after Express processes them. Express views support multiple layout and CSS preprocessor engines. In this book, we will focus on Jade for HTML and Stylus for CSS.

Node HTTP/HTTPS API

Express is built on top of Node's HTTP/HTTPS API. When one hears something like that, often it so happens that the underlying API is insulated by the framework, but it is not the case in Express. The Node HTTP/HTTPS API is very much accessible from the Express framework—the `req` and `res` objects are extensions of the `req` and `res` socket objects in a plain vanilla Node HTTP server.

So, anytime you feel the need to hack a little deeper, you can go ahead and work on the original Node objects and their properties and methods.

While we are at it, I would like to stress the point that not only is the HTTP/HTTPS API available for Express, but the whole of Node API is available from Express. Reading up the complete Node documentation will help you become a more efficient Express developer—you will understand the underlying mechanism better, write better middleware and modules for your apps, and have more control over the framework.

Downloading the example code

You can download the example code fi les for all Packt books you have purchased from your account at `http://www.packtpub.com`. If you purchased this book elsewhere, you can visit `http://www.packtpub.com/support` and register to have the files e-mailed directly to you

Summary

In this chapter, we learned about the core concepts and components in Express. We were also introduced to some example Express code, which prepared us for what we will be coming across in the coming chapters.

We now know what the omnipresent `req`, `res`, and `next` objects are in an Express application. We learned how to write middlewares and Node modules to extend the capability of our Express app. We are now ready get hands-on with a real Express app.

In the next chapter, we will get coding and create our first Express app. We will start from the very basics and learn about the various aspects that make up an Express app.

2
Your First Express App

This chapter is about understanding the core structural and functional aspects of an Express app. We will start with a very basic app and proceed to make it gradually more complex by introducing the components of a relatively advanced Express app one after another.

This chapter is essential to develop a very good understanding of what an Express app is made up of, and how it works.

You will learn the following in this chapter:

- How to create a very basic Express app
- How to define basic routes and handle them
- How to use views
- How to include CSS, JavaScript, and images in the app
- How to use middleware
- How to include Node modules in the app
- How to log requests to the app
- How to configure the app
- How to run the app in different modes

Your first Express app

The best way to learn any new technology is to try it out using some practical examples. So, let's go ahead and build an Express app and find out how it works.

To ensure our experiments do not mess up our filesystem, let's create a directory named `express-app` in your home directory and build our app there:

```
$ cd ~
$ mkdir express-app
$ cd express-app
```

The app directory is ready and we can start building our first Express app.

The Express manifest file

In *Chapter 1, What is Express?*, we learned that Express apps are actually Node modules, which means our app also would need a manifest file. So, create a file named `package.json` in the app directory.

The `package.json` file can have more than a dozen fields, but for the sake for brevity, let's keep it minimal. Here is what it should look like:

```
{
  "name": "test-app",
  "version": "0.0.1",
  "private": true,
  "scripts": {
    "start": "node app"
  },
  "dependencies": {
    "express": "3.2.6",
    "jade": "*"
  }
}
```

The fields used in the manifest file are explained in the following table:

Field	Description
`name`	The name of the module.
`version`	The version of the module.
`private`	Indicates whether this module is meant to be published on the `npm` registry or not.
`scripts`	`npm` commands for the module. In our case, we will support only the `start` command. `npm start` will call the node app.
`dependencies`	A list of other Node modules this module depends on. In our case, we specify that it depends on only two modules: `express` at version 3.0.1 and the latest version of `jade`.

For an interactive guide to all the possible fields in a `package.json` file, visit `http://package.json.nodejitsu.com/`.

We have the manifest file ready now. Executing the `npm install` command in the directory will install all the dependencies in the directory:

```
$ npm install
```

You will see a huge wall of scrolling text, that's the dependencies being installed. Once it's done, you will find a new directory named `node_modules` in the directory; that's where all the dependencies are installed. Because the directory is created and its contents generated by the `npm install` command, you can safely delete this directory any time you need to for whatever reason, and regenerate it using the same command.

With the dependencies installed, we are now ready to start building out first Express app—from scratch.

Each Express app hosts its own copy of Express framework in a directory named `express`, under the `node_modules` directory. You can safely play around with the framework files without affecting other apps. If you ever mess something up, just reinstall it by running `npm install` in the app directory.

A very basic Express app

Let's create a very basic Express app to get us started. Create a file called `app.js` and put the following code in it:

```
// Include the Node HTTP library
var http = require('http');
// Include the Express module
var express = require('express');
// Create an instance of Express
var app = express();

// Start the app
http.createServer(app).listen(3000, function() {
  console.log('Express app started');
});

// A route for the home page
app.get('/', function(req, res) {
  res.send('Welcome!');
});
```

The app will listen on port `3000` and will have a very limited functionality. It will print "Welcome" when you load its home page, and return a 404 error for all other requests.

HTTP 404 and 500 error handling is built into the `router` middleware. The details about customizing these error handlers are covered in *Chapter 4, Response from the Server*.

You might have noticed that the route in the app is defined after the code for starting the server, but it works anyway. Isn't it shocking that it should even work?

The reason it works is because routes are defined on the `app` object, which is passed to the HTTP API as a reference—any time you make a change on the `app` object, it is reflected on the server.

Logically, it makes sense to defined the route first and then pass the `app` object to the HTTP API, but I did afterwards to disruptively bring it to your attention about how the `app` object is passed to the HTTP API—it is passed as a reference and its methods and properties can be accessed any time. Routes can be defined dynamically, but once defined cannot be redefined.

So much for its being the most important middleware; `router` wasn't even mentioned in the app. So how does this app work at all?

The mere definition of a route implicitly adds the `router` middleware at that point of the middleware stack. This feature might be acceptable in simple apps like ours, but in more complex apps, you will need to include the `router` middleware explicitly, to ensure the proper order of middlewares in the stack. You will learn more about Express middleware in an upcoming section.

Starting and stopping the app

Since Express apps are Node programs, starting an Express app is similar to executing a Node program. In our case, the program resides in a file named `app.js`, so this is how you will start the server:

```
$ node app
> Express app started
```

To stop the server, press *Ctrl* + *C*.

Analyzing the output

Start the app and load `http://localhost:3000` on your browser to see the output:

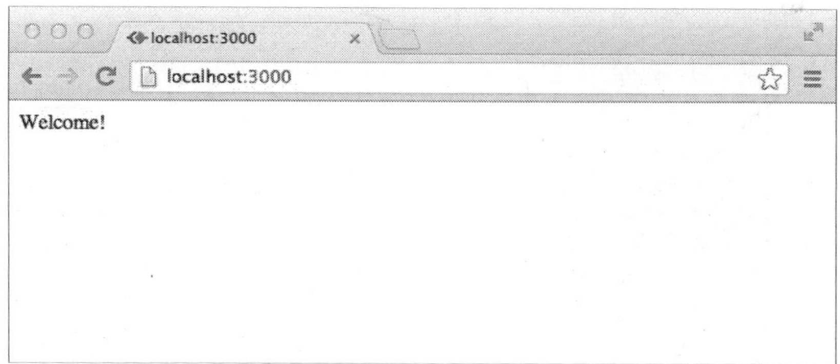

If you view the source of the web page and you will find that the server has sent the response in plain text.

How about sending some HTML in the response?

To send HTML response, just change `res.send('Welcome!')` to `res.send('<h1>Welcome!</h1>')`, and restart the server. Refresh the page to see the HTML formatted text, as shown in the following screenshot:

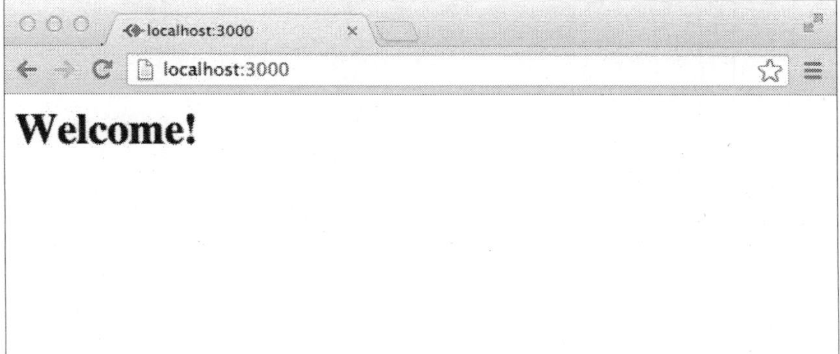

> For the changes made in application files to reflect, you need to restart the server. This can be a tedious process; you can make it easier for yourself by using **supervisor**, a Node module that will watch the application files and restart the server when any one of them changes. You can learn more about supervisor at `https://github.com/isaacs/node-supervisor`.

Now, how do we send a whole HTML page?

Express apps have a special component called **views**, wherein you write the necessary HTML using a templating language, which helps in separating HTML from the core app. Also, any changes made in the views will be reflected in the HTML output without requiring the server to be restarted.

Express app with views

Let's rewrite the app to use views. The view files can reside in any conveniently named directory on the filesystem, but it makes sense to have it right in the application directory.

So, let go ahead and create a directory for our views, named `views`:

```
$ mkdir views
```

Now create two view files in the `views` directory: one named `index.jade` for the home page, another named `hello.jade` for the hello web page.

The first thing you might notice about the view files is that they have the `.jade` extension. This unfamiliar extension might make it look a little intimidating, but you will discover that it is very intuitive once you start using it.

> Note that Jade is just one of the many templating languages that is supported by Express. It is not mandatory to use Jade with Express. However, we focus on it especially because it was created keeping Express in mind, and is a natural fit for it. If you want to learn more about Jade, you can take a quick look at *Chapter 5, The Jade Templating Language*.
>
> Express supports all templating languages that work with Node. It is just a matter of installing the right module and configuring your app to use it.

Let's familiarize ourselves with Jade by creating the content of the view files:

Here is the content for `index.jade`:

```
html
  head
      title Welcome
  body Welcome!
```

And here is the content for `hello.jade`:

```
html
  head
```

```
    title Hello
  body
    b Hello!
```

As you can notice, indentation is the key in Jade. You use consistent space- or tab-based indentations to nest HTML elements. We don't need to use the overly verbose HTML opening and closing tags. There is much more to Jade than this, but for now, you should be good to go with it. You will learn more about Jade in *Chapter 5, The Jade Templating Language*.

Make sure to consistently use spaces or tabs for indentation, or else Jade will throw an error.

Let's update `app.js` to use our newly created views. The following code is commented well to help you understand what each relevant line of code is doing:

```
var http = require('http');
var express = require('express');
var app = express();

// Set the view engine
app.set('view engine', 'jade');
// Where to find the view files
app.set('views', './views');

// A route for the home page - will render a view
app.get('/', function(req, res) {
  res.render('index');
});

// A route for /say-hello - will render a view
app.get('/say-hello', function(req, res) {
  res.render('hello');
});

app.get('/test', function(req, res) {
  res.send('this is a test');
});

http.createServer(app).listen(3000, function() {
  console.log('App started');
});
```

In the updated `app.js`, we have declared that we will be using the Jade templating engine, and have specified the `views` directory for Jade. You can see we are using `res.render()` for two of the routes to render views.

For a matched route, `res.render()` will look for the view in the `views` directory and render it accordingly

Restart the server and load `http://localhost:3000`, `http://localhost:3000/say-hello`, and `http://localhost:3000/test` in the browser to see the new additions made to the app.

If you view the source of these web pages, you will find that the ones using views have generated complete HTML.

Make some changes in the view files and refresh the browser to see the changes. You don't need to restart the app to see the changes made in the view files, they are reflected instantly when you refresh the browser.

So far you have only seen a preview of Jade, you will learn much more in *Chapter 5, The Jade Templating Language*. Till then, let's continue understanding an Express app better.

A public directory for the app

We are now quite close to having a fully functional website, albeit a simple one. What remain now are CSS, JavaScript, images, and other files for the app. Where do we keep these files?

Express has a middleware called `static`, using which we can mark a directory in the filesystem for serving static files for the app. Any file kept in these directories can be directly accessed via the browser.

This is how you use the `static` middleware to set a directory for static resources:

```
app.use(express.static('./public'));
```

It is worth noting that you can set multiple static directories, if you need to:

```
app.use(express.static('./public'));
app.use(express.static('./files'));
app.use(express.static('./downloads'));
```

Let's create a static directory named `public` and use it for our static content:

```
$ mkdir public
$ mkdir public/images
```

```
$ mkdir public/javascripts
$ mkdir public/stylesheets
```

These directory names are chosen by convention, you can name them anything you want; as long as the static directory is set, they will work as expected. However, it is a good idea to stick to what I suggested, because those names are very commonly used by web developers around the world.

Create a nice looking image named `logo.png` and keep it in the `images` directory. I am using the following Packt logo:

Create a file named `main.js` in the `javascripts` directory with the following content:

```
window.onload = function() {
  document.getElementById('smile').innerHTML = ':)';
};
```

Create a file named `style.css` in the `stylesheets` directory with the following content:

```
#content {
  width: 220px;
  margin: 0 auto;
  text-align: center;
  border: 1px solid #ccc;
  box-shadow: 0 3px 4px #ccc;
  padding: 5px;
}
```

Update `index.jade` to include the newly added files:

```
html
  head
    title Welcome
    script(src='javascripts/main.js')
    link(rel='stylesheet', href='stylesheets/style.css')
  body
    #content
      img(src='images/logo.png')
      p WELCOME
      #smile
```

Update `app.js` to set a static directory:

```
var http = require('http');
var express = require('express');
var app = express();

app.set('view engine', 'jade');
app.set('views', './views');

// Mark the public dir as a static dir
app.use(express.static('./public'));

app.get('/', function(req, res) {
  res.render('index');
});

http.createServer(app).listen(3000, function() {
  console.log('App started');
});
```

Restart the app and load the home page:

Congrats! Your first full-fledged Express app is up and running.

Auto-generating an Express app

The process of creating the manifest file, the `app.js` file, the views, and other directories and files can become a tedious chore as we start to work on multiple projects. To automate this process, we can use the `express` command-line tool.

To refresh you memory, we first encountered the `express` command-line tool while learning how to install Express. We were told that it generates Express app skeletons; now we have a fairly good idea what it might do.

Using its help option (`-h`), let's ask express how it works and what its options are:

```
$ express -h

  Usage: express [options] [directory]

  Options:

    -h, --help          output usage information
    -V, --version       output the version number
    -s, --sessions      add session support
    -e, --ejs           add ejs engine support (defaults to jade)
    -J, --jshtml        add jshtml engine support (defaults to jade)
    -H, --hogan         add hogan.js engine support
    -c, --css <engine>  add stylesheet <engine> support (less|stylus)
(defaults to plain css)

  Directory:

An optional directory where to create the app (defaults to pwd)
```

I have added the description for the `[directory]` parameter myself, it is missing in the official `express` help screen. If you don't specify a directory, the current directory is assumed to be the target directory.

So, the `express` command accepts some options and an optional directory to auto-generate an app. Let's create a new app using our newfound knowledge of `express`:

```
$ express --sessions ~/auto-express
create : /Users/yaapa/auto-express
create : /Users/yaapa/auto-express/package.json
create : /Users/yaapa/auto-express/app.js
create : /Users/yaapa/auto-express/public
create : /Users/yaapa/auto-express/public/javascripts
```

```
create : /Users/yaapa/auto-express/public/images
create : /Users/yaapa/auto-express/public/stylesheets
create : /Users/yaapa/auto-express/public/stylesheets/style.css
create : /Users/yaapa/auto-express/views
create : /Users/yaapa/auto-express/views/layout.jade
create : /Users/yaapa/auto-express/views/index.jade
create : /Users/yaapa/auto-express/routes
create : /Users/yaapa/auto-express/routes/index.js
create : /Users/yaapa/auto-express/routes/user.js
install dependencies:
  $ cd /Users/yaapa/auto-express && npm install

run the app:
  $ node app
```

You can see that the command created a bunch of file and directories, and exited with the instructions for installing the dependencies and starting the app.

On running the `npm install` command in the app directory, you will see the familiar dependency installation process seen earlier at the beginning of the chapter. Once the dependency installation process is completed, take a look at the content of the directory:

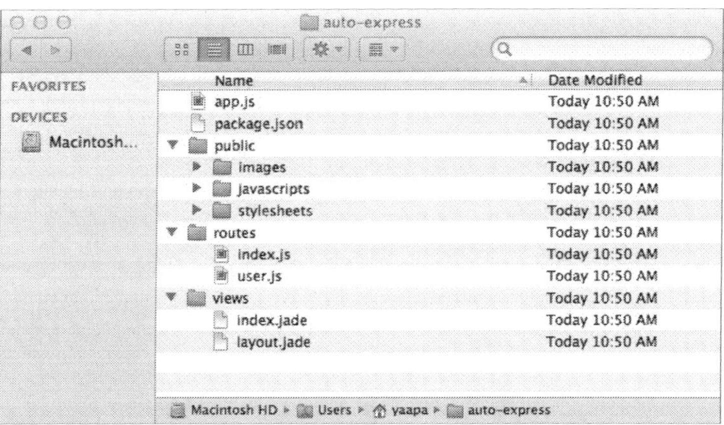

That's exactly what we already created! Well, almost, except for a new directory named `routes`, and a file named `layout.jade` in the `views` directory. Don't be too bothered by them at this stage. The `routes` directory will become clear to you in *Chapter 3, Understanding Express Routes* and the `layout.jade` file in *Chapter 5, The Jade Templating Language*.

So now you know, you don't have to sweat creating all the files and directories for each of your apps, the `express` command is there to take care of them for you.

> The auto-generated files, directories, and the directory structure created by the `express` command is called a **skeleton app**. It is called so, because it is a barebones app, upon which you can start building your app.

Manually creating the files and directories is the way to go when starting to learn Express, but once you know what you are doing and start working on real projects, you should use the `express` command to save yourself a lot of time.

One thing to note about express-generated files, directories, and the directory structure is that, they are just suggestions—you are free to modify them to fit your needs anytime and however you want them.

> Even though we created a new app directory called `auto-express`, to maintain continuity, all upcoming examples will be continued in our original app directory `express-app`.

Empowering Express with middlewares

In *Chapter 1, What is Express?*, we learned about Express middlewares and saw how to create one. Now, let's go find out how to include one in our app. Remember we use `app.use()` for including middlewares.

Though we can write our own middlewares, we will focus on using one of the middlewares that comes bundled with Express.

For your reference, the following is the list of the middlewares that are available in Express, by default:

Middleware	Description
`router`	The app's routing system
`logger`	Log requests to the server
`compress`	gzip/deflate support on the server
`basicAuth`	Basic HTTP authentication
`json`	Parse `application/json`
`urlencoded`	Parse `application/x-www-form-urlencoded`

Middleware	Description
`multipart`	Parse multipart/form-data
`bodyParser`	Parse request body. Bundles `json`, `urlencoded`, and multipart middlewares together
`timeout`	Request timeout
`cookieParser`	Cookie parser
`session`	Session support
`cookieSession`	Cookie-based sessions
`methodOverride`	HTTP method support
`responseTime`	Show server response time
`static`	Static assets directory for the website
`staticCache`	Cache for the static middleware
`directory`	Directory listing
`vhost`	Enable `vhost`
`favicon`	Favicon for the website
`limit`	Limit the size of request body
`query`	The `GET` query parser
`errorHandler`	Generate HTML-formatted stack trace of errors in the server

So there you have it, the list of middlewares available to you by default. For this example, we will use the `responseTime` middleware.

Modify `app.js` to use this middleware:

```
var http = require('http');
var express = require('express');
var app = express();

app.set('view engine', 'jade');
app.set('views', './views');

app.use(express.static('./public'));
// Add the responseTime middleware
app.use(express.responseTime());

app.get('/', function(req, res) {
  res.render('index');
```

```
});

http.createServer(app).listen(3000, function() {
  console.log('App started');
});
```

Restart the server. Load up the app in the browser and look at the HTTP response headers in any network traffic analyzer (I am using Google Chrome's Developer Tool):

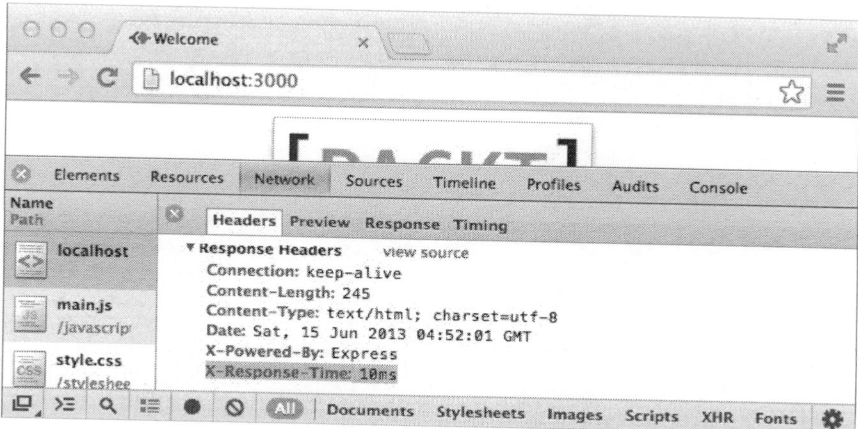

When we enable the `responseTime` middleware, Express sends the time taken to process a request in the HTTP response header (**X-Response-Time**). You can see it highlighted in the preceding screenshot.

Now let's try using the `errorHandler` middleware. For test purposes, we will generate an error in the home page's route handler by calling an undefined function. According to the `errorHandler` middleware's description, it should format the error into a nice looking HTML page.

Edit `app.js` to include the middleware and generate the error:

```
var http = require('http');
var express = require('express');
var app = express();

app.set('view engine', 'jade');
app.set('views', './views');

app.use(express.static('./public'));
app.use(express.responseTime());
```

```
// Add the errorHander middleware
app.use(express.errorHandler());

app.get('/', function(req, res) {
  // Call an undefined function to generate an error
  fail();
});

http.createServer(app).listen(3000, function() {
  console.log('App started');
});
```

Restart the server and load the home page, you'll get an error message, as shown in the following screenshot:

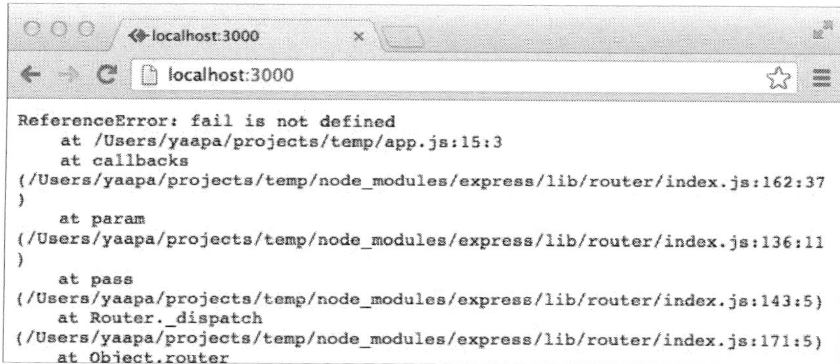

The output doesn't look like an HTML page at all! In fact, you can confirm it is not HTML by looking at the source code. Why is the `errorHandler` middleware not working?

In the beginning of this chapter, I mentioned that unless you add the `router` middleware explicitly, it will be added at the point where a route is defined. The most important requirement of `errorHandler` is that it should be added after the `router` middleware. No wonder it didn't work as expected.

So now it makes sense to explicitly add the `router` middleware if we want to use `errorHandler` productively. You never know which other middleware might require `router` to be defined beforehand, so let's modify `app.js` to include the `router` middleware explicitly:

```
var http = require('http');
var express = require('express');
```

```
var app = express();

app.set('view engine', 'jade');
app.set('views', './views');

app.use(express.static('./public'));
app.use(express.responseTime());
// Explicitly add the router middleware
app.use(app.router);
// Add the errorHander middleware
app.use(express.errorHandler());

app.get('/', function(req, res) {
  // Call an undefined function to generate an error
  fail();
});

http.createServer(app).listen(3000, function() {
  console.log('App started');
});
```

Now restart the server, refresh the home page, and see the output:

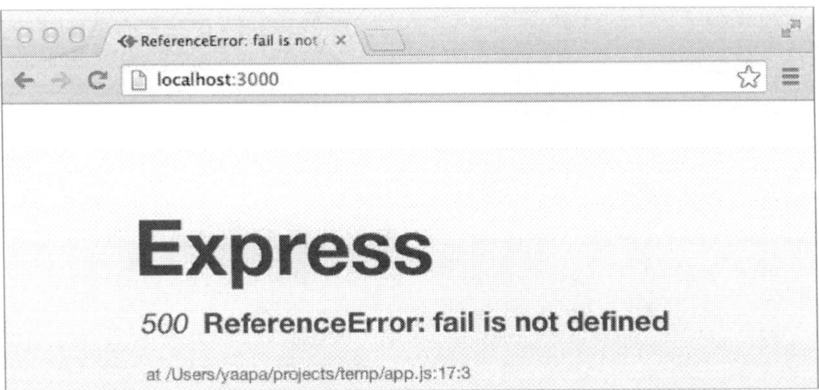

This time the `errorHandler` middleware is doing what it is supposed to do.

Like `errorHandler`, you can use other middlewares whenever you might need them. By default, Express doesn't do a lot, but using its middleware you can make it do many other useful things.

As we saw earlier, you can write you own middleware, if you want. Anything you want to do with `req` and the `res` object, middleware is the way to go.

Empowering Express with Node modules

Express does not come packed with a huge bunch of built-in libraries to perform tasks that are beyond a basic website. Express is very minimal. But that does not mean that it is not capable of performing complex tasks.

You have a huge collection of Node modules on the npm registry that can be easily plugged in to your app and used for performing all sorts of tasks in the app.

In *Chapter 1, What is Express?*, we were introduced to Node modules, and we learned how to write them. We also found out that they can be used to modularly extend the power and capability of Express.

You could write your own Node modules to accomplish many things, but anything you are trying to achieve, probably there is an excellent open source Node module out there already. You just need to find the right module, install it, and use it in your app.

> The npm registry/network in a publicly available online resource where Node developers publish their Node modules. These modules are installed using the `npm` command.
>
> You can find a huge list of Node modules at `https://github.com/joyent/node/wiki/Modules`. From the command line, you can use the `npm search` command or use a module such as `npm-search` or `npm-research` to search for modules of your interest.

Let's find out how we can install and use a Node module from the NPM registry. We will install a `.ini` file parsing module named `iniparser` and use it in our app:

```
$ npm install iniparser
npm WARN package.json application-name@0.0.1 No README.md file found!
npm http GET https://registry.npmjs.org/iniparser
npm http 304 https://registry.npmjs.org/iniparser
iniparser@1.0.5 node_modules/iniparser
```

The module has been installed successfully. Create `config.ini` in the app directory with the following content:

```
title = My Awesome App
port = 3000
message = You are awesome!
```

You might have guessed it already, we are going to use this as the configuration file for our app.

Now edit `app.js` to include the module and use it in our app:

```
var http = require('http');
var express = require('express');
var app = express();
// Load the iniparser module
var iniparser = require('iniparser');
// Read the ini file and populate the content on the config object
var config = iniparser.parseSync('./config.ini');

app.set('view engine', 'jade');
app.set('views', './views');

app.use(express.static('./public'));
app.use(express.responseTime());
app.use(app.router);
app.use(express.errorHandler());

app.get('/', function(req, res) {
  // Pass two config variables to the view
  res.render('index', {title:config.title, message:config.message});
});

http.createServer(app).listen(config.port, function() {
  console.log('App started on port ' + config.port);
});
```

While we are at it, we'd like to increase the complexity of the view a little bit more, so go ahead and edit `index.jade` too:

```
html
  head
    title #{title}
    script(src='javascripts/main.js')
    link(rel='stylesheet', href='stylesheets/style.css')
  body
    #content
      img(src='images/logo.png')
      p WELCOME
      p #{message}
      #smile
```

Restart the app and load it in the browser to see the "drastic" changes:

So, you see Express does not come with the inherent ability to parse `.ini` files, but has the extensibility to be able to do almost anything with the correct Node module, because of which we can parse `.ini` files and use one in our app.

Logging requests to the App

Express comes with a built-in logging module called **logger**, it can be a very useful tool while you are developing the app. You enable it like any other Express module:

```
app.use(express.logger());
```

Without any options, the `logger` middleware will log a detailed log. You can customize the details with the following tokens in the `format` option of the `logger` middleware:

Token	Content
`:req[header]`	The specific HTTP header of the request
`:res[header]`	The specific HTTP header of the response
`:http-version`	The HTTP version
`:response-time`	How long it took to generate the response
`:remote-addr`	The user agent's IP address
`:date`	Date and time of request

Token	Content
`:method`	The HTTP method used for making the request
`:url`	The requested URL
`:referrer`	The URL that referred the current URL
`:user-agent`	The user-agent signature
`:status`	The HTTP status

And this is how you specify the log format using the tokens:

```
app.use(express.logger({ format: ':remote-addr :method :url' }));
```

After adding the `logger` middleware, you can see the log details in the console, when requests are made to the app:

```
127.0.0.1 GET /
127.0.0.1 GET /favicon.ico
```

By default the logger outputs the log to the console. We can make it log to a file by specifying the `stream` option, as shown here:

```
var http = require('http');
var express = require('express');
var fs = require('fs');
var app = express();

app.use(express.logger({
  format: 'tiny',
  stream: fs.createWriteStream('app.log', {'flags': 'w'})
}));

...
```

The `logger` middleware supports four predefined log formats: `default`, `short`, `tiny`, and `dev`. You can specify one of them this way:

```
app.use(express.logger('dev'));
```

If you need to quickly check some aspects of the requests that are being made, the `logger` middleware is the way to go.

Using a configuration file

We actually don't need to use an `.ini` file for configuring our apps, as shown in a previous example. The purpose of the example was just to show you how to use a Node module, not the recommended practice.

As a side effect of how `require()` works, Node supports JSON-based configuration files by default. Create a file with a JSON object describing the configurations, save it with a `.json` extension, and then load it in the app file using `require()`.

[It is important to ensure that the file extension is `.json` and the JSON object confirms to the JSON specification, or else it will throw an error.]

Here is an example of a JSON-based config file:

```
{
  "development": {
    "db_host": "localhost",
    "db_user": "root",
    "db_pass": "root"
  },

  "production": {
    "db_host": "192.168.1.9",
    "db_user": "myappdb",
    "db_pass": "!p4ssw0rd#"
  }
}
```

This is how you would load it:

```
var config = require('./config.json')[app.get('env')];
```

Now the environment-specific configuration details will be available on the `config` object. Assuming your app is running on production, the following would be the result of using the configuration file:

```
console.log(config.db_host); // 192.168.1.9
console.log(config.db_user); // myappdb
console.log(config.db_pass); // !p4ssw0rd#
```

A configuration file is not mandatory for an Express app, but it helps in making it modular and maintainable.

Setting and getting application options

An Express application has a set of predefined application variables that are used to configure various options of the app. These variables are used for setting various dynamic aspects of the app and can be set using the `app.set()` method. So far we have used two of them:

```
app.set('view engine', 'jade');
app.set('views', './views');
```

The values of application variables can be retrieved using the corresponding `app.get()` method.

The following table lists all the options that can be configured in an Express app:

Option	Purpose
`env`	The environment the app is running on. Not recommended to set manually. You will read more about this in the next section.
`trust proxy`	Enables reverse proxy.
`jsonp callback name`	Callback name for JSONP requests.
`json replacer`	The JSON replacer callback.
`json spaces`	The amount of space for indenting JSON responses.
`case sensitive routing`	Makes route names case-sensitive.
`strict routing`	Trailing slash at the end of a route name should be treated as separate from that without.
`view cache`	Cache views. Enabled in production by default.
`view engine`	The engine for processing view files.
`views`	The directory of view files.

Express in different environments

In a software release process, we designate systems for development, UAT, staging, production, and so on for different stages of product release. Technically, these contexts of application execution are called **environments**.

It is very common that we want our software to execute differently on different environments. For example, in a development environment, we would like to see a very verbose detail about any error our software might encounter, but we might not want to do so in the production environment. Express has a very simple mechanism to let us do that. Let's find out how it works.

Express' `app.get('env')` method returns the current environment of the app. Based on this value, you can configure your app to use different middlewares, Node modules, and so on; effectively changing the behavior of the app based on the environment.

Before we go about configuring our app based on its environment, let's find out how `app.get('env')` works.

When an Express app starts, it looks for an environment variable called `NODE_ENV` at the `process.env` object, if it finds it, the value of `NODE_ENV` is assigned to the app variable `env`, or else it is assigned `development`. This app variable can be read by `app.get()` and written by `app.set()`.

If `NODE_ENV` is not set on your machine, it will be assumed to be a development environment. If it is really intended to be used as a development machine, you need not set any value, but for anything else, especially production, it is required to set the environment name.

This is how you create the environment variable and set it to `production`:

```
$ export NODE_ENV=production
```

Now when you start your app, it will detect the `NODE_ENV` environment variable and kick in the production mode.

However, the variable will only last as long as your current shell session does. To "permanently" mark a system as a production environment, it makes sense to set the `NODE_ENV` value to `production` every time you log in. This is how you can do that:

```
$ echo export NODE_ENV=production >> ~/.bash_profile
```

Now, this system will be marked as a production server.

As I mentioned earlier, you can overwrite the value of the `env` app variable using `app.set()` anytime you want. Using this capability, you can hardcode the environment name in your application file. But it is not recommended; one unfortunate day when you misspell the environment name or forget to change it, you will be in big trouble.

Let the system tell Express what environment it is executing in, don't let the app decide what environment it is executing in.

Now what happens if you want to see how the app would behave in the production environment, while still being on the development server? Do you have to upload the app to the production server? That doesn't sound effective at all, does it?

Worry not. You can temporarily set any value to `NODE_ENV` in your shell, and start the app, to simulate any environment you want. This is how you can do so:

```
$ NODE_ENV=production node app
```

Now the app will run in production mode. The good thing about this method is that the value of `NODE_ENV` lasts only as long as the app is running. Once you stop the app and start it the regular way, it will run in the system's default mode again.

Now that we know how `app.get('env')` works, let's configure our app to work according to the environment it is in.

Edit `app.js` to conditionally add or enable features according to the environment, as shown in the following code:

```
var http = require('http');
var express = require('express');
var app = express();
var iniparser = require('iniparser');
var config = iniparser.parseSync('./config.ini');

app.set('view engine', 'jade');
app.set('views', './views');

app.use(express.static('./public'));
app.use(express.responseTime());
app.use(app.router);

// Setup for production environment
if ('production' == app.get('env')) {
  app.get('/', function(req, res) {
    res.render('index', {title:config.title, message:config.message});
  });
}

// Setup for development environment
if ('development' == app.get('env')) {
  app.use(express.errorHandler());
  app.get('/', function(req, res) {
    res.send('development mode test');
  });
}
```

```
// Common setup for all the environments
app.get('/test', function(req, res) {
  res.send('works on all environment');
});

http.createServer(app).listen(config.port, function() {
  console.log('App started on port ' + config.port);
});
```

Restart the server and see how the app behaves according to environment type.

In production mode:

```
$ NODE_ENV=production node app
```

In test mode:

```
$ NODE_ENV=test node app
```

Setting up the app according to the environment was previously implemented in another way using the `app.configure()` method. It is deprecated now and included, as follows, just for reference:

```
// Setup for production environment
app.configure('production', function() {
  app.get('/', function(req, res) {
    res.render('index', {title:config.title, message:config.message});
  });
});

// Setup for development environment
app.configure('development', function() {
  app.use(express.errorHandler());
  app.get('/', function(req, res) {
    res.send('development mode test');
  });
});

// Common setup for all the environments
app.configure(function() {
  app.get('/test', function(req, res) {
    res.send('works on all environment');
  });
});
```

Edit the `app.js` file accordingly and restart the server to see the configurations kick in again.

With the last example, you have come to a point where you can configure your Express app using all possible methods. If you have been paying good attention, your Express basics should be rock solid now.

Summary

In this chapter, we learned how to create a fairly complete Express app from the ground up. We started by demonstrating the fact that Express are Node modules. Then we went on to create a simple app, upon which we added more and more components and features to make it more complex. By the end of the exercise, we had an app that could run on different modes depending on the environment.

We now have a good amount of knowledge to make sense of an auto-generated Express app.

Since routes are the public interfaces to an app, they make it a natural topic to focus on next. We will learn in detail about routes in Express in the next chapter.

3

Understanding Express Routes

This chapter is about routes—the request interfaces to your application. We have seen and used some routes in the previous chapters, but there is much more to routes than creating one by giving a name and including a callback function to handle the request.

In this chapter, you will get a deeper insight into how routes work and how you can customize them to make your application more flexible and powerful.

You will learn the following in this chapter.

- How to define routes
- How to handle routes
- How to organize routes

What are Routes?

Routes are URL schema, which describe the interfaces for making requests to your web app. Combining an HTTP request method (a.k.a. **HTTP verb**) and a path pattern, you define URLs in your app.

Each route has an associated route handler, which does the job of performing any action in the app and sending the HTTP response.

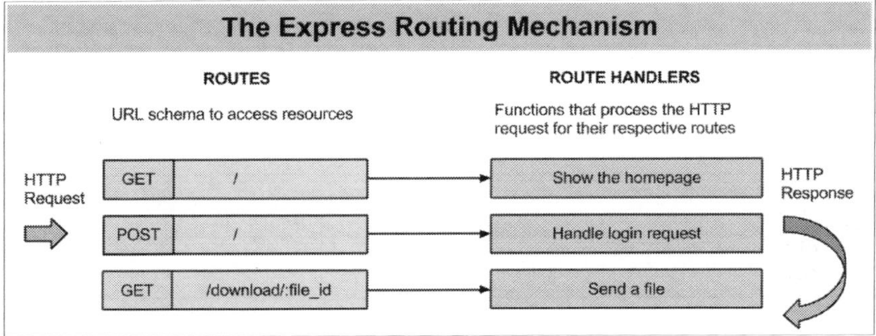

Routes are defined using an HTTP verb and a path pattern. Any request to the server that matches a route definition is routed to the associated route handler.

Route handlers are middleware functions, which can send the HTTP response or pass on the request to the next middleware in line. They may be defined in the app file or loaded via a Node module.

A quick introduction to HTTP verbs

The HTTP protocol recommends various methods of making requests to a Web server. These methods are known as HTTP verbs. You may already be familiar with the `GET` and the `POST` methods; there are more of them, about which you will learn in a short while.

Express, by default, supports the following HTTP request methods that allow us to define flexible and powerful routes in the app:

- `GET`
- `POST`
- `PUT`
- `DELETE`
- `HEAD`
- `TRACE`
- `OPTIONS`
- `CONNECT`
- `PATCH`
- `M-SEARCH`
- `NOTIFY`

- `SUBSCRIBE`
- `UNSUBSCRIBE`

GET, POST, PUT, DELETE, HEAD, TRACE, OPTIONS, CONNECT, and PATCH are part of the Hyper Text Transfer Protocol (HTTP) specification as drafted by the **Internet Engineering Task Force (IETF)** and the World Wide Web Consortium (W3C). M-SEARCH, NOTIFY, SUBSCRIBE, and UNSUBSCRIBE are specified by the UPnP Forum.

There are some obscure HTTP verbs such as LINK, UNLINK, and PURGE, which are currently not supported by Express and the underlying Node HTTP library.

Routes in Express are defined using methods named after the HTTP verbs, on an instance of an Express application: `app.get()`, `app.post()`, `app.put()`, and so on. We will learn more about defining routes in a later section.

Even though a total of 13 HTTP verbs are supported by Express, you need not use all of them in your app. In fact, for a basic website, only GET and POST are likely to be used.

Revisiting the router middleware

This chapter would be incomplete without revisiting the `router` middleware.

The `router` middleware is very special middleware. While other Express middlewares are inherited from Connect, `router` is implemented by Express itself. This middleware is solely responsible for empowering Express with Sinatra-like routes.

Connect-inherited middlewares are referred to in Express from the `express` object (`express.favicon()`, `express.bodyParser()`, and so on). The `router` middleware is referred to from the instance of the Express app (`app.router`).

To refresh your memory, we learned in *Chapter 2, Your First Express App*, that if the `router` middleware is not explicitly added in the middleware stack, it is added at the point where a route is defined for the first time. To ensure predictability and stability, we should explicitly add `router` to the middleware stack:

```
app.use(app.router);
```

The `router` middleware is a middleware system of its own. The route definitions form the middlewares in this stack. Meaning, a matching route can respond with an HTTP response and end the request flow, or pass on the request to the next middleware in line. This fact will become clearer as we work with some examples in the upcoming sections.

Though we won't be directly working with the `router` middleware, it is responsible for running the whole routing show in the background. Without the `router` middleware, there can be no routes and routing in Express.

Defining routes for the app

From the examples in *Chapter 1, What is Express?* and *Chapter 2, Your First Express App*, we know how routes and route handler callback functions look like. Here is an example to refresh your memory:

```
app.get('/', function(req, res) {
  res.send('welcome');
});
```

Routes in Express are created using methods named after HTTP verbs. For instance, in the previous example, we created a route to handle `GET` requests to the root of the website. You have a corresponding method on the `app` object for all the HTTP verbs listed earlier.

Let's create a sample application to see if all the HTTP verbs are actually available as methods in the `app` object:

```
var http = require('http');
var express = require('express');
var app = express();

// Include the router middleware
app.use(app.router);

// GET request to the root URL
app.get('/', function(req, res) {
  res.send('/ GET OK');
});

// POST request to the root URL
app.post('/', function(req, res) {
  res.send('/ POST OK');
});
```

```
// PUT request to the root URL
app.put('/', function(req, res) {
  res.send('/ PUT OK');
});

// PATCH request to the root URL
app.patch('/', function(req, res) {
  res.send('/ PATCH OK');
});

// DELETE request to the root URL
app.delete('/', function(req, res) {
  res.send('/ DELETE OK');
});

// OPTIONS request to the root URL
app.options('/', function(req, res) {
  res.send('/ OPTIONS OK');
});

// M-SEARCH request to the root URL
app['m-search']('/', function(req, res) {
  res.send('/ M-SEARCH OK');
});

// NOTIFY request to the root URL
app.notify('/', function(req, res) {
  res.send('/ NOTIFY OK');
});

// SUBSCRIBE request to the root URL
app.subscribe('/', function(req, res) {
  res.send('/ SUBSCRIBE OK');
});

// UNSUBSCRIBE request to the root URL
app.unsubscribe('/', function(req, res) {
  res.send('/ UNSUBSCRIBE OK');
});

// Start the server
http.createServer(app).listen(3000, function() {
  console.log('App started');
});
```

We did not include the HEAD method in this example, because it is best left for the underlying HTTP API to handle it, which it already does. You can always do it if you want to, but it is not recommended to mess with it, because the protocol will be broken unless you implement it as specified.

The browser address bar isn't capable of making any type of request, except GET requests. To test these routes we will have to use HTML forms or specialized tools. Let's use **Postman**, a Google Chrome plugin for making customized requests to the server.

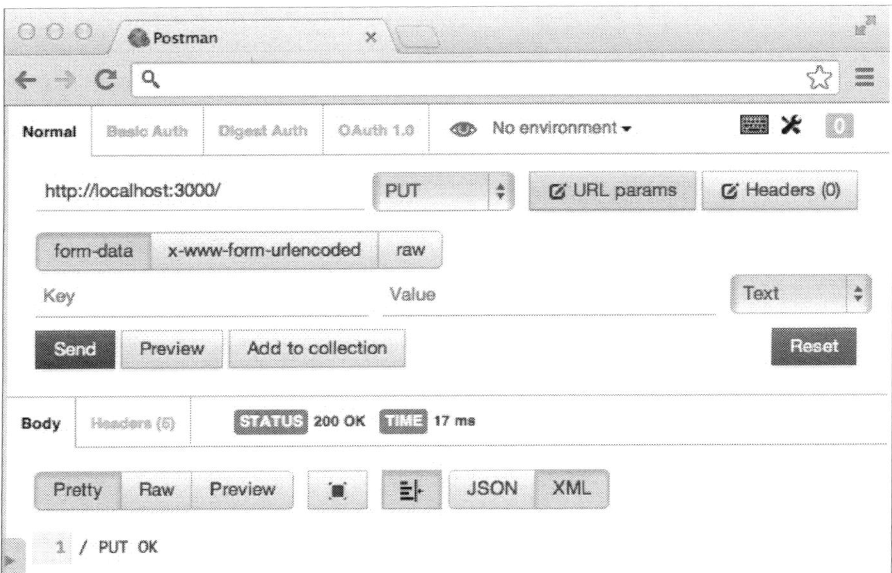

We learned that route definition methods are based on HTTP verbs. Actually, that's not completely true, there is a method called app.all() that is not based on an HTTP verb. It is an Express-specific method for listening to requests to a route using any request method:

```
app.all('/', function(req, res, next) {
  res.set('X-Catch-All', 'true');
  next();
});
```

Place this route at the top of the route definitions in the previous example. Restart the server and load the home page. Using a browser debugger tool, you can examine the HTTP header response added to all the requests made to the home page, as shown in the following screenshot:

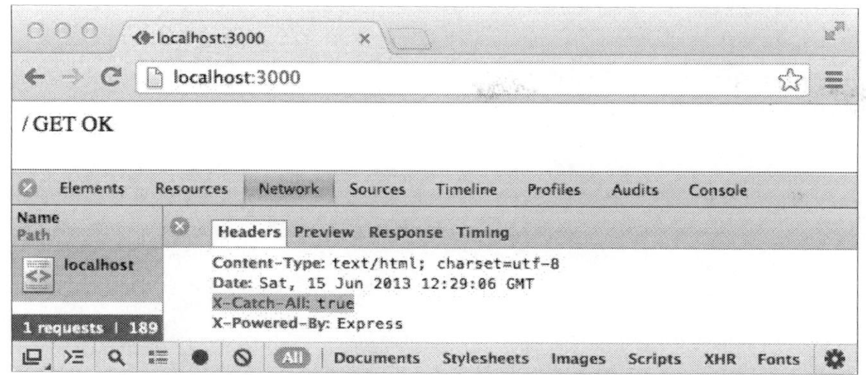

Something similar can be achieved using a middleware. But the `app.all()` method makes it a lot easier when the requirement is route specified.

Route identifiers

So far we have been dealing exclusively with the root URL (/) of the app. Let's find out how to define routes for other parts of the app.

Routes are defined only for the request path. `GET` query parameters are not and cannot be included in route definitions.

Route identifiers can be string or regular expression objects.

String-based routes are created by passing a string pattern as the first argument of the routing method. They support a limited pattern matching capability. The following example demonstrates how to create string-based routes:

```
// Will match /abcd
app.get('/abcd', function(req, res) {
  res.send('abcd');
});

// Will match /acd
app.get('/ab?cd', function(req, res) {
  res.send('ab?cd');
});
```

```
// Will match /abbcd
app.get('/ab+cd', function(req, res) {
  res.send('ab+cd');
});

// Will match /abxyzcd
app.get('/ab*cd', function(req, res) {
  res.send('ab*cd');
});

// Will match /abe and /abcde
app.get('/ab(cd)?e', function(req, res) {
  res.send('ab(cd)?e');
});
```

[The characters `?`, `+`, `*`, and `()` are subsets of their Regular Expression counterparts.

The hyphen (`-`) and the dot (`.`) are interpreted literally by string-based route identifiers.]

There is another set of string-based route identifiers, which is used to specify named placeholders in the request path. Take a look at the following example:

```
app.get('/user/:id', function(req, res) {
  res.send('user id: ' + req.params.id);
});

app.get('/country/:country/state/:state', function(req, res) {
  res.send(req.params.country + ', ' + req.params.state);
}
```

The value of the named placeholder is available in the `req.params` object in a property with a similar name.

Named placeholders can also be used with special characters for interesting and useful effects, as shown here:

```
app.get('/route/:from-:to', function(req, res) {
  res.send(req.params.from + ' to ' + req.params.to);
});

app.get('/file/:name.:ext', function(req, res) {
  res.send(req.params.name + '.' + req.params.ext.toLowerCase());
});
```

The pattern-matching capability of routes can also be used with named placeholders. In the following example, we define a route that makes the `format` parameter optional:

```
app.get('/feed/:format?', function(req, res) {
  if (req.params.format) { res.send('format: ' + req.params.format); }
  else { res.send('default format'); }
});
```

Routes can be defined as regular expressions too. While not being the most straightforward approach, regular expression routes help you create very flexible and powerful route patterns.

Regular expression routes are defined by passing a regular expression object as the first parameter to the routing method.

Do not quote the regular expression object, or else you will get unexpected results.

Using regular expression to create routes can be best understood by taking a look at some examples.

The following route will match `pineapple`, `redapple`, `redaple`, `aaple`, but not `apple`, and `apples`:

```
app.get(/.+app?le$/, function(req, res) {
  res.send('/.+ap?le$/');
});
```

The following route will match anything with an `a` in the route name:

```
app.get(/a/, function(req, res) {
  res.send('/a/');
});
```

You will mostly be using string-based routes in a general web app. Use regular expression-based routes only when absolutely necessary; while being powerful, they can often be hard to debug and maintain.

Order of route precedence

Like in any middleware system, the route that is defined first takes precedence over other matching routes. So the ordering of routes is crucial to the behavior of an app. Let's review this fact via some examples.

In the following case, `http://localhost:3000/abcd` will always print "abc*"

, even though the next route also matches the pattern:

```
app.get('/abcd', function(req, res) {
  res.send('abcd');
});

app.get('/abc*', function(req, res) {
  res.send('abc*');
});
```

Reversing the order will make it print "abc*":

```
app.get('/abc*', function(req, res) {
  res.send('abc*');
});

app.get('/abcd', function(req, res) {
  res.send('abcd');
});
```

The earlier matching route need not always gobble up the request. We can make it pass on the request to the next handler, if we want to.

In the following example, even though the order remains the same, it will print "abc*" this time, with a little modification in the code.

Route handler functions accept a third parameter, commonly named `next`, which refers to the next middleware in line. We will learn more about it in the next section:

```
app.get('/abc*', function(req, res, next) {
  // If the request path is /abcd, don't handle it
  if (req.path == '/abcd') { next(); }
  else { res.send('abc*'); }
});

app.get('/abcd', function(req, res) {
  res.send('abcd');
});
```

So bear it in mind that the order of route definition is very important in Express. Forgetting this will cause your app behave unpredictably. We will learn more about this behavior in the examples in the next section.

How to handle routes

When a request is made to the server, which matches a route definition, the associated callback functions kick in to process the request and send back a response. These callback functions are responsible for the dynamic behavior of the app; without them routes would simply be dumb interfaces that do nothing at all.

So far, we have been dealing with a single callback function for a route, but a route can have more than one callback function.

As mentioned earlier, the Express routing system is also built around the middleware concept—each route handler has the capability to send a response or pass on the request to the next route-handling middleware in the current or the next matching route.

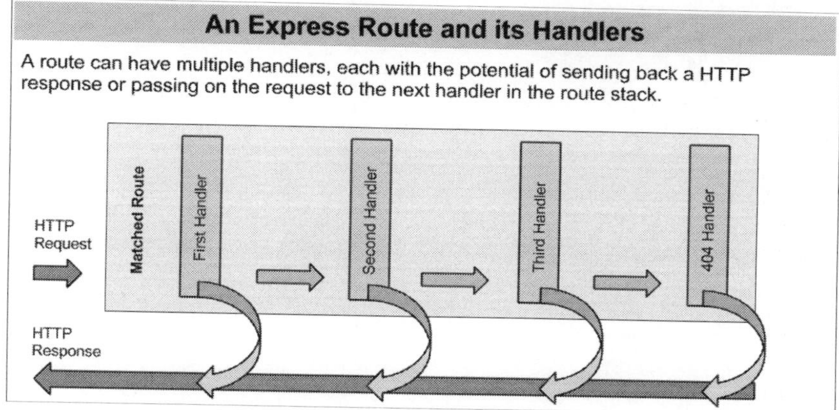

All of a sudden route handling sounds a little more complicated than what we assumed earlier, doesn't it? Let's find out if it is so.

By now, we are all familiar with how a route definition looks like:

```
app.get('/', function(req, res) {
  res.send('welcome');
});
```

We have been using a single callback function in all our examples so far. So, where do the other callback functions come in and what do they do?

In *Chapter 1, What is Express?*, we saw the `next()` function being called to execute the next middleware in the stack. Route handlers, being middlewares, also have access to the `next` object, which happens to be the next callback function in the line. To make the `next` object available to the callback function, pass it along with the `req` and the `res` objects to it:

```
app.get('/', function(req, res, next) {
  next();
});
```

If there is no matching callback function after the current callback function, `next` refers to the built-in 404 error handler, and it will be triggered when you call it.

This is how you specify multiple callbacks for a route:

```
app.get('/',

  function(req, res, next) {
    res.send('one');
  },

  function(req, res, next) {
    res.send('two');
  },

  function(req, res) {
    res.send('three');
  }
);
```

Try guessing what the response will be. Will the server print all of them, or "one" or, "three"?

The server will print just "one". The act of doing a `res.send()` or `send.render()` or other similar method terminates the flow of the request then and there; the request is not passed on to any other middleware.

So, how do we specify multiple callbacks for a route, and use them all at the same time? Call the `next()` function from the callback, without calling any of the methods that terminates the request flow. Here is an example:

```
app.get('/',

  function(req, res, next) {
    res.set('X-One', 'hey!');
    next();
```

```
    },

    function(req, res, next) {
      res.set('X-Two', 'ho!');
      next();
    },

    function(req, res) {
      res.send("Let's go!");
    }
  );
```

This route handler stack is composed of three callbacks. The first two add two additional HTTP headers. You can see that the two functions have successfully added the HTTP headers, and the third is printed to the browser:

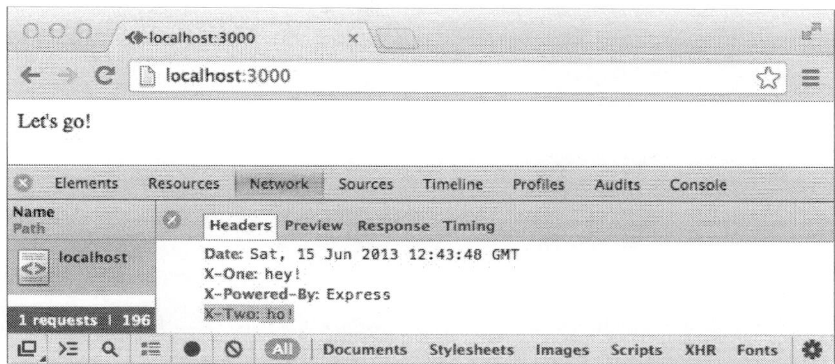

HTTP headers are protocol-level information sent by an HTTP server in response to a request. They are not displayed by the browser, but can be seen using a traffic analyzer or web development tools such as Firebug and Chrome Developer Tool.

The callback functions can be passed in an array too. The following modification to the code will result in the same response, similar to the one shown in the preceding example, from the server:

```
var one = function(req, res, next) {
  res.set('X-One', 'hey!');
  next();
};

var two = function(req, res, next) {
```

```
  res.set('X-Two', 'ho!');
  next();
};

app.get('/', [one, two], function(req, res) {
  res.send("Let's go!");
});
```

You can achieve the same thing again by defining multiple routes for a route path. This is not really recommended, but it will help you to better understand how routes work:

```
app.get('/', function(req, res, next) {
  res.set('X-One', 'hey!');
  next();
});

app.get('/', function(req, res, next) {
  res.set('X-Two', 'ho!');
  next();
});

app.get('/', function(req, res) {
  res.send('three');
});
```

Showing the various ways of assigning callbacks to a route is not a recommendation in any manner; it is just to show you the possibilities. You may most likely stick with the single callback approach, but knowing the fact that you can assign more than one callback to a router in various ways will give you flexibility and and power if the need ever arises.

How to organize routes

So far, our routes and their handlers have been written right in the app file. It might work for small apps, but is not practical for bigger projects. After a certain level of complexity in our app, we will need to organize your routes.

So what is the Express way of organizing routes?

The Express way of organizing routes is—chose what works best for you. Express does not force, recommend, or suggest any form of routing pattern on its developers. However, it provides the capability to implement any sort of routing pattern you may want to implement for your app.

There are three popular ways of organizing routes in an Express app; let's explore them.

Using Node modules

In *Chapter 1, What is Express?*, we learned that Node modules can be of any JavaScript object type, including functions. Since route handlers are function, we can modularize our app by using Node nodules to define our route handlers.

Create a directory named `routes` to keep our route handlers. In the directory, create two basic Node modules: `index.js` and `users.js`.

Here is the content for `index.js`:

```
exports.index = function(req, res){
  res.send('welcome');
};
```

And, here is the content for `users.js`:

```
exports.list = function(req, res){
  res.send('Amar, Akbar, Anthony');
};
```

Now, update the `app.js` file to include our route handlers:

```
var express = require('express');
var http = require('http');
var app = express();

// Load the route handlers
var routes = require('./routes');
var user = require('./routes/users');

// Add router middleware explicitly
app.use(app.router);

// Routes
app.get('/', routes.index);
app.get('/users', user.list);

http.createServer(app).listen(3000, function(){
  console.log('App started');
});
```

Start the app and load `http://localhost:3000` and `http://localhost:3000/users` on the browser to see the results.

Now our route handlers reside in separate Node modules, making our app a little more modular. Can the app be made even more modular?

How about moving also the route definitions out of the `app.js` file?

In our new scheme, the `routes` directory will be called `handlers`. So, go ahead and rename `routes` to `handlers`. The modules need not be renamed or edited.

Create a new file called `routes.js` in the app directory. This file will be responsible for loading the route handlers and defining the routes. Here is the content for the file:

```
// Load the route handlers
var routes = require('./handlers');
var user = require('./handlers/users');

module.exports = function(app) {

  // Define the routes
  app.get('/', routes.index);
  app.get('/users', user.list);

};
```

Now modify the `app.js` file to incorporate the new changes we have made:

```
var http = require('http');
var express = require('express');
var app = express();

// Explicitly add the router middleware
app.use(app.router);

// Pass the Express instance to the routes module
var routes = require('./routes')(app);

http.createServer(app).listen(3000, function() {
  console.log('App started');
});
```

Restart the app and reload `http://localhost:3000` and `http://localhost:3000/users` to see the functionality intact.

There you go, an even more modular app.

This method of organizing the routes used the basic module loading capability of Node to introduce modularity in the app. There are other methods of route organization, which introduce a layer of abstraction to create routing patterns. Let's explore two of them: namespaced routing and resourceful routing.

Namespaced routing

Take a look at the following set of route definitions:

```
app.get('/articles/', function(req, res) { … });
app.get('/articles/new', function(req, res) { … });
app.get('/articles/edit/:id', function(req, res) { … });
app.get('/articles/delete/:id', function(req, res) { … });
app.get('/articles/2013', function(req, res) { … });
app.get('/articles/2013/jan/', function(req, res) { … });
app.get('/articles/2013/jan/nodejs', function(req, res) { … });
```

As the number of routes and their path segments grow, you will start to wonder if there is any way to organize them better, and flatten the growing pyramid of repeating strings in the path names.

How about the ability to define root paths and defining other routes based on it? That would cut down the repetitive text in path names, right?

Namespaced routing is just about that. You define the routes in your app based on a namespace, which happens to be the root of the path, relative to which other routes are defined.

You will have a better understanding about how namespaced routing works if we re-write the preceding routes using namespaced routing, so let's do that.

Express does not support namespaced routing by default, but it is very easy to enable support by installing a Node module called `express-namespace`:

```
$ npm install express-namespace
```

Now, edit `app.js` to include `express-namespace` and redefine the routes using namespaces:

```
var http = require('http');
var express = require('express');

// express-namespace should be loaded before app is instantiated
var namespace = require('express-namespace');
var app = express();
```

```
app.use(app.router);

app.namespace('/articles', function() {

  app.get('/', function(req, res) {
    res.send('index of articles');
  });

  app.get('/new', function(req, res) {
    res.send('new article');
  });

  app.get('/edit/:id', function(req, res) {
    res.send('edit article ' + req.params.id);
  });

  app.get('/delete/:id', function(req, res) {
    res.send('delete article ' + req.params.id);
  });

  app.get('/2013', function(req, res) {
    res.send('articles from 2013');
  });

  // Namespaces can be nested
  app.namespace('/2013/jan', function() {

    app.get('/', function(req, res) {
      res.send('articles from jan 2013');
    });

    app.get('/nodejs', function(req, res) {
      res.send('articles about Node from jan 2013');
    });
  });

});

http.createServer(app).listen(3000, function() {
  console.log('App started');
});
```

Restart the app and load the following URLs in your browser to see namespaced routing in action:

- `http://localhost:3000/articles/`
- `http://localhost:3000/articles/edit/4`
- `http://localhost:3000/articles/delete/4`
- `http://localhost:3000/articles/2013`
- `http://localhost:3000/articles/2013/jan`
- `http://localhost:3000/articles/2013/jan/nodejs`

Namespaces support all the pattern matching and regular expression support we read earlier, so the flexibility and power of defining routes is not compromised by using namespaced routing.

Although we used `app.get()` for defining all the routes for the sake of simplicity, it is not recommended to actually do so in production. Doing so can leave the resources of your app open to deletion via the most basic and unexpected actions, even by web spiders. Use `app.delete()` instead, with authentication.

Resourceful routing

Another popular routing pattern is an object-oriented approach called resourceful routing. The idea behind resourceful routing is to create routes based on actions available on objects called resources on the server.

Resources are entities such as users, photos, forums, and so on on the server.

Resourceful routes are defined using a recommended combination of HTTP verbs and path patterns. Corresponding methods are defined in the route handling Node module to perform the necessary actions in the server.

The following table illustrates resourceful routing for a resource called `users` in the server:

HTTP Verb	Path	Module Method	Description
`GET`	`/users`	`index`	Lists users
`GET`	`/users/new`	`new`	The form to create a new user

HTTP Verb	Path	Module Method	Description
POST	/users	create	Processes new user form submission
GET	/users/:id	show	Shows user with ID :id
GET	/users/:id/edit	edit	Form to edit user with ID :id
PUT	/users/:id	update	Processes user edit form submission
DELETE	/users/:id	destroy	Deletes user with ID :id

Resourceful routing is not supported by Express by default. However, enabling it is as easy as installing a Node module named `express-resource`:

```
$ npm install express-resource
```

Next, we need to create a Node module to handle the resourceful routes. Create a file called `users.js` and implement the resourceful methods in it:

```
exports.index = function(req, res) {
  res.send('index of users');
};

exports.new = function(req, res) {
  res.send('form for new user');
};

exports.create = function(req, res) {
  res.send('handle form for new user');
};

exports.show = function(req, res) {
  res.send('show user ' + req.params.user);
};

exports.edit = function(req, res) {
  res.send('form to edit user ' + req.params.user);
};

exports.update = function(req, res) {
  res.send('handle form to edit user ' + req.params.user);
};

exports.destroy = function(req, res) {
  res.send('delete user ' + req.params.user);

};
```

Now modify `app.js` to use the `express-resource` module and load the route-handling Node module:

```
var http = require('http');
var express = require('express');
// Load express-resource BEFORE app is instantiated
var resource = require('express-resource');

var app = express();

app.use(app.router);

// Load the resourceful route handler
app.resource('users', require('./users.js'));

http.createServer(app).listen(3000, function() {
  console.log('App started');
});
```

Start the app and load the following URLs in your browser to see the resourceful route handlers print the assigned messages:

- `http://localhost:3000/users`
- `http://localhost:3000/users/new`
- `http://localhost:3000/users/7`
- `http://localhost:3000/users/7/edit`

For `POST`, `PUT`, and `DELETE` routes, you will have to use a form or a tool such as Postman to see the results:

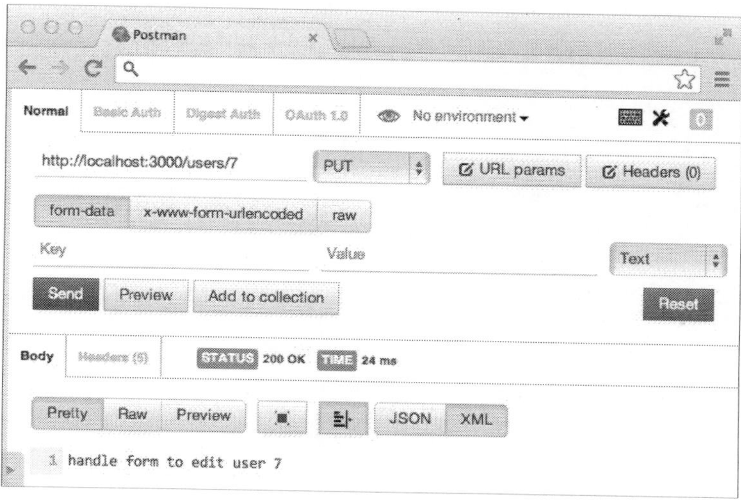

In a real-world application, `POST`, `PUT`, and `DELETE` methods are called using HTML forms. We are limited to `GET` examples by the browser address bar which just supports `GET` requests. You will learn more about forms and how to make other type of HTTP requests in *Chapter 6, The Stylus CSS Preprocessor*.

So you can see, in resourceful routing you just have to specify the resource name and implement the resourceful methods. The task of creating the routes is handled by the underlying `express-resource` module.

Making a choice

Express aims to be an unopinionated web development framework. Apart from the very basics, it does not impose any software development patterns on the developers. At the same time it is so flexible that you can set up Express to nearly work like Ruby on Rails, plain old PHP, Kohana, Django, or any other web development framework you might have heard about.

The Express ideology of not being opinionated applies to routing too. Routes can be implemented and organized in numerous ways. Some people like to define the routes right in the app file, some like to keep them in a Node module, some like to go the namespaced way, and some prefer the resourceful approach.

There is no one recommended way to implement routes in your app. Each app is different and the needs are different. Resourceful routing in a simple app would be overkill, while not planning the routes for a CMS application would be very bad software development practice.

It is best to be aware about the possible ways of implementing and organizing routes in an Express app, and pick the best according to the need of the application.

Summary

In this chapter, we learned about routes and route handlers in great detail. We can now define flexible routes and route handlers. An important insight we got was the fact that route handers are a middleware system of their own. We also learned the various ways of organizing our routes and route handlers.

Now that we know how to define and handle routes, in the next chapter let's find out how to send various types of responses from the server.

4

Response From the Server

This chapter is about understanding how web servers respond to HTTP requests and how it works in Express. We will cover the details of the response process and learn how to serve different kinds of content in Express.

You will learn the following in this chapter:

- The basics of HTTP response format
- How to set HTTP status code in Express
- How to set HTTP headers in Express
- How to serve different kinds of content in Express

A primer on HTTP response

To understand the types of response Express is capable of generating and have a better control over them, it is important that you have some technical understanding about the underlying HTTP protocol's response format. So, let's go over it real quick and cover the basics.

> HTTP response is a small part of the much bigger HTTP protocol. As a web developer it is an added advantage if you have a good understanding of the protocol you are working with. You can read about the HTTP protocol in detail at `http://www.w3.org/Protocols/`.

The data sent by an HTTP server in response to a request is called an **HTTP response message**. It is composed of a status code, headers, and optional associated data, which is technically referred to as the body of the message.

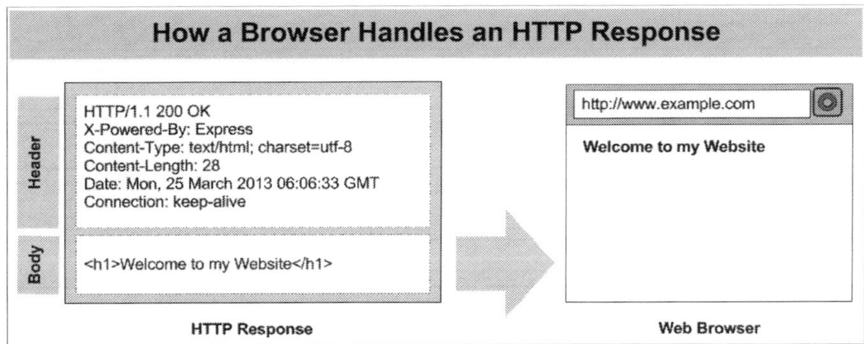

The body is presented to the user as plain text, rendered HTML, image, file download, and so on. The status code and the headers are hidden from a regular user, but the browser requires them to process the body appropriately.

HTTP status codes

You might be familiar with 404 and 500 errors already. These error names are derived from the HTTP status code used to convey the errors.

404 and 500 are examples from the number of HTTP status codes that can be sent by the server to the client. Although there are a number of HTTP status codes, the reason you don't get to see them all is, because these codes are targeted at the user agent and the exchange takes place in the background.

> An HTTP user agent is any software that a user makes use of to make requests to a web server. In most cases, the user agent happens to be a web browser, so we will be using the terms "user agent" and "browser" interchangeably in this book.

All responses from an HTTP server come with an associated status code. The most common among them is 200—the code for a successful request. Here is an example of a 200 HTTP status code:

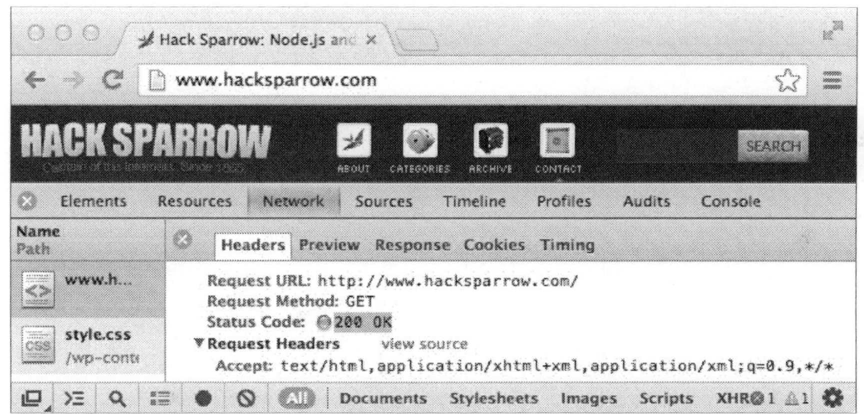

Although not visible to a the regular user, the HTTP status code sent by the server can be seen in the **Network** tab of most browser debugging tools.

Here is an example of a **404** status code sent by the server when requested for a non-existent resource:

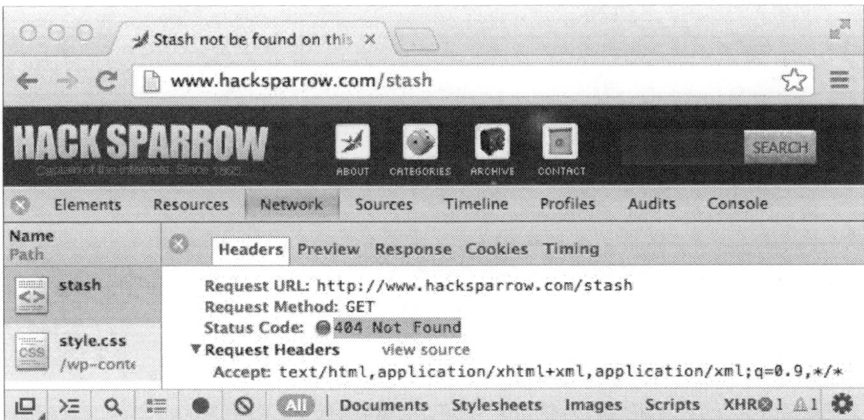

As mentioned a while ago, HTTP status codes are not limited to just 200, 404, and 500; there are many more used for conveying many different kinds of messages.

Since we are working with Express, which is an HTTP server, it makes sense to be the aware about all the HTTP status codes, even if we don't get into the finer details about them.

Following is a list of all the HTTP status codes for your information and general knowledge:

It is beyond the scope of this book to get into all the details of HTTP status code, but you can find them all at `http://www.w3.org/Protocols/rfc2616/rfc2616-sec10.html`.

1xx

The 1xx series of status codes is classified as **Informational**, and is used for conveying provisional response from the server.

The available codes in this series are: 100, 101, and 102.

2xx

The 2xx series of status codes is classified as **Success**, and is used for conveying a successful request for a resource on the server.

The available codes in this series are: 200, 201, 202, 303, 204, 205, 206, 207, 208, 250, and 226.

3xx

The 3xx series of status codes is classified as **Redirection**, and is used for information by the user agent about taking additional action to retrieve the requested resource.

The available codes in this series are: 300, 301, 302, 303, 304, 305, 306, 307, and 308.

4xx

The 4xx series of status codes is classified as **Client Error**, and is used for informing the user agent of its erroneous requests to the server.

The available codes in this series are: 400, 401, 402, 403, 404, 405, 406, 407, 408, 409, 410, 411, 412, 413, 414, 415, 416, 417, 422, 423, 424, 425, 426, 428, 429, 431, 444, 449, 450, 451, 452, 453, 454, 455, 456, 457, 458, 459, 460, 461, 462, 494, 495, 496, 497, and 499.

5xx

The 5xx series of status codes is classified as **Server Error**, and is used for informing the user agent that the server has encountered an error because of which the request was not fulfilled.

The available codes in this series are: 500, 501, 502, 503, 504, 505, 506, 507, 508, 509, 510, 511, 551, 598, and 599.

HTTP response headers

HTTP response headers (often referred to as just headers) are key-value pairs sent after the HTTP status code in a HTTP message. These headers are used for conveying various important pieces of information from the server to the user agent.

The following is an example of headers sent by a web server:

```
X-Powered-By: Express
Accept-Ranges: bytes
ETag: "819254-1356021445000"
Date: Mon, 11 Mar 2013 21:19:05 GMT
Cache-Control: public, max-age=0
Last-Modified: Thu, 20 Dec 2012 16:37:25 GMT
Content-Type: image/gif
Content-Length: 819254
Connection: keep-alive
```

HTTP headers, like HTTP status codes, are targeted at the user agent, rather than the user, so they are also not visible to a regular user. However, they can be seen using network traffic analyzers and browser debugging tools such as Firebug and Chrome Developer Tool.

The HTTP protocol specifies a standard set of headers and possible values, which can be set in a message; however, there is no technical restriction on the actual implementation. Having said that, it is recommended to follow the standards to ensure the app works in a predictable manner.

Media types

Media type describes the kind of data that is being transferred over the Internet protocol; in our case it would be the HTTP protocol.

You might already be familiar with terms such as `text/html`, `multipart/form-data`, `text/plain`, and so on, those are examples of description of media types.

> Media Type is also commonly referred to as **MIME Type** or **Content Type**. You can read more about them at `http://www.iana.org/assignments/media-types`.

Whenever an HTTP server sends a response, it also specifies what kind of data it is sending via the **Content-Type** header, which is shown in the following screenshot:

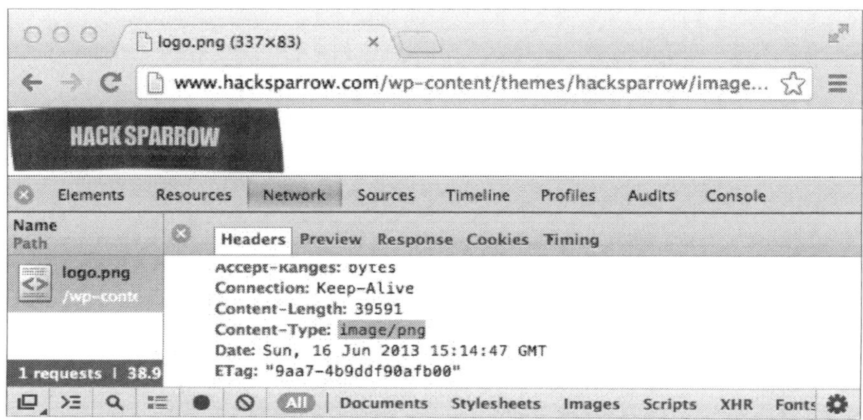

The `Content-Type` header can have an optional parameter, which specifies the encoding for the data being transferred. On the Web, this parameter is most commonly applicable to string data, such as plain text, HTML, and JSON:

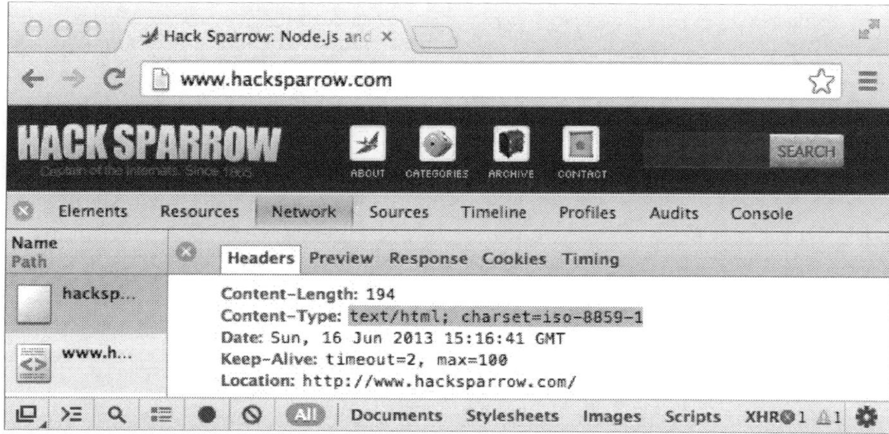

UTF-8 is the most popular encoding format on the Web, and is the default in JavaScript, Node, and Express.

HTTP response in Express

Now that we have covered the basics of HTTP response in general, let's find out if it works in Express.

By now, we already know how a simple HTTP response can be generated in Express—by setting up a route and a handler for it:

```
app.get('/', function(req, res) {
  res.send('welcome');
});
```

Let's examine the response for this response.

Express can send an HTTP response using one of its response methods: `res.send()`, `res.json()`, `res.jsonp()`, `res.sendfile()`, `res.download()`, `res.render()`, or `res.redirect()`. If none of them is called, the request will be left hanging till the connection times out.

If more than one response methods are specified in a route handler, only the first method will take effect, the rest will generate non-fatal, run-time errors.

Start the app, load the homepage, and look at the response headers using a browser-debugging tool:

```
HTTP/1.1 200 OK
X-Powered-By: Express
Content-Type: text/html; charset=utf-8
Content-Length: 7
Date: Sat, 09 Mar 2013 15:55:24 GMT
Connection: keep-alive
```

The HTTP status is set to **200 OK**, the content type is set to **text.html; charset=utf-8**, and a bunch of other HTTP headers have been set. Express does all of these for you, automatically for successful requests.

It is not limited to successful results only, Express also handles 404 errors for you. Try making a request to a non-existent URL on your local machine, for example, `http://localhost:3000/foo`, and examine the response headers:

```
HTTP/1.1 404 Not Found
X-Powered-By: Express
Content-Type: text/plain
```

```
Date: Sat, 09 Mar 2013 17:54:22 GMT
Connection: keep-alive
Transfer-Encoding: chunked
```

In fact, Express does all that is expected from any decent web server. Naturally, it handles 500 errors too. Modify the home page handler to cause a runtime error:

```
app.get('/', function(req, res) {
  // Call an undefined function
  error();
});
```

Restart the app, load the homepage, and examine the response headers again:

```
HTTP/1.1 500 Internal Server Error
X-Powered-By: Express
Content-Type: text/plain
Content-Length: 938
Date: Sat, 09 Mar 2013 18:06:13 GMT
Connection: keep-alive
```

So Express takes care of setting the right HTTP status code and headers for the requests made to it, and we really don't have to do anything much at all. It is all well and good, but being curious hackers, we start to wonder if there are ways to customize the HTTP status code and the headers. Can we?

Setting the HTTP status code

Setting the HTTP status code is as easy as passing a number to the `res.status()` method. Let's look at some examples of to find out how `res.status()` works.

`res.status()` alone is not enough to handle the response. It needs to be used in conjunction with one of the Express HTTP response methods, such as `res.send()`, `res.render()`, and so on, or else the request will be left hanging.

In the following example, we send a status code of 404 even though the home page route actually exists. If we hadn't specified 404, Express would have sent a status code of 200:

```
app.get('/', function(req, res) {
  // Set the status
  res.status(404);
  // Specify the body
  res.send('forced 404');
});
```

And in this example, we send a 500 status code:

```
app.get('/', function(req, res) {
  res.status(500);
  res.send('forced 500');
});
```

`res.status()` is a chainable method, meaning we can do things like the following:

```
app.get('/', function(req, res) {
  // Status and body in one line
  res.status(404).send('not found');
});
```

Among the HTTP response methods, `res.send()`, `res.json()`, and `res.jsonp()` are capable of specifying the HTTP status code themselves, without the help of `res.status()`. When a status code is not specified, a default of 200 is assigned.

Here are some examples showing how it works using `res.send()`:

```
app.get('/', function(req, res) {
  res.send('welcome');
});
```

When a number alone is passed to `res.send()`, it is assumed to be the intended status code. The server will just send the status code and the basic headers, with no body:

```
app.get('/', function(req, res) {
  res.send(404);
});
```

It is your responsibility to pass the proper HTTP status code to the response methods; Express won't check the validity of the number. Whatever you pass will be sent to the user agent.

And of course, you can set the status code and the body at the same time, like so:

```
app.get('/', function(req, res) {
  res.send(404, 'not found');
});
```

For `res.render()`, `res.sendfile()`, and `res.download()`, you will need to specify the status code using the `res.status()` method, or else it will default to 200:

```
app.get('/', function(req, res) {
```

```
    res.status(404);
    res.render('index', {title: 'Express'});
  });
```

And as shown earlier, `res.status()` can be chained with the appropriate response method to accomplish everything in a single line:

```
  app.get('/', function(req, res) {
    res.status(404).render('index', {title: 'Express'});
  });
```

It is important to note that `res.render()`, `res.sendfile()`, and `res.download()` do not accept a single numeric parameter and send a response with just the status code.

Setting HTTP headers

Express provides a very easy interface for setting HTTP headers in the response message. You pass two parameters to the `res.set()` method; the first parameter is the header name and the second parameter is its value.

In the following example, we set a standard HTTP header along with two custom headers:

```
  app.get('/', function(req, res) {
    // status is optional, it defaults to 200
    res.status(200);
    res.set('Content-Type', 'text/plain; charset=us-ascii');
    res.set('X-Secret-Message', 'not really secret');
    res.set('X-Test', 'OK');
    res.send('welcome');
  });
```

The custom headers along with the standard HTTP headers can be seen in a web debugger tool.

> Note that HTTP header key names are case-insensitive from the browser's context—`Content-Type` and `content-type` are both interpreted as the same thing. It is also worth noting that the standard practice of setting custom HTTP header is to use a key prefixed with `X-`, as shown in the example.

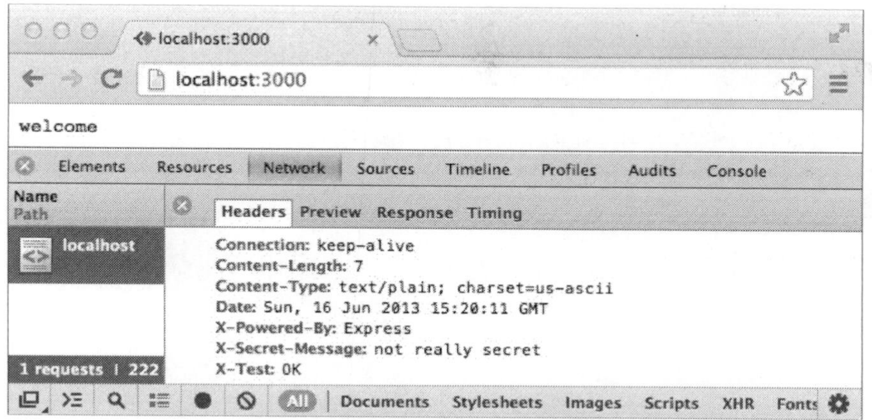

If the process of individually setting the headers seems tedious to you, you can use the alternative approach of passing an object to `res.set()` instead. The key-value pair in the object will be assigned as the header and its value in the HTTP response message:

```
app.get('/', function(req, res) {
  res.set({
    'Content-Type': 'text/plain; charset=us-ascii',
    'X-Secret-Message': 'not really secret',
    'X-Test': 'OK'
  });
  res.send('welcome');
});
```

Very related to setting HTTP headers, Express provides a `res.charset` property, which can be used to set the value of the optional `Content-Type` header. This property is best used when you just want to change the charset of the default `Content-Type` of `text/html`.

The following code will set the `Content-Type` header to `text/html; charset=us-ascii`:

```
app.get('/', function(req, res) {
  res.charset = 'us-ascii';
  res.send('welcome');
});
```

Now that we have covered setting the HTTP status code and headers, it is about time that we started learning about sending stuff to the users that they can actually see and interact with.

Sending data

The component of an HTTP response message, which users can generally see and interact with, is called the body of the message. The body can come in many different forms—as HTML, plain text, images, binary files, CSS files and so on—and the `Content-Type` header is exclusively used to convey to the user agent what sort of data it is dealing with.

Let's find out how different kinds of data can be served from an Express application.

Plain text

One may wonder if we actually need to dedicate a section on how to send plain text from Express. We will soon find out whether it was worth it or not.

Let's create a very simple route handler for the home page route. Our intention is to see the HTML tags as is in the browser:

```
app.get('/', function(req, res) {
  res.send('<h1>welcome</h1>');
});
```

Start the app, load the homepage, and analyze the output:

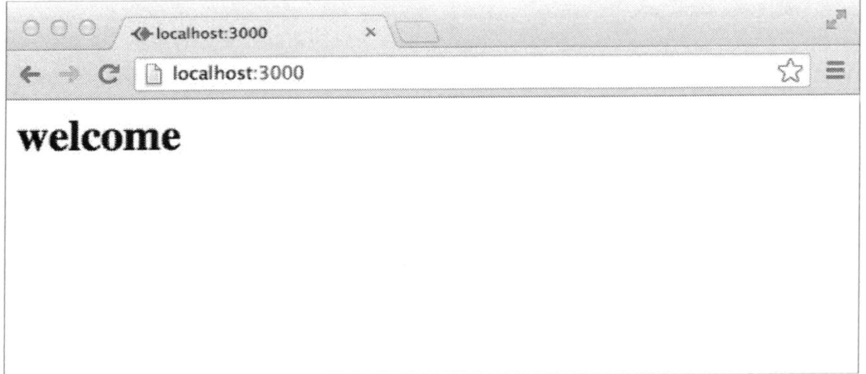

The browser actually rendered the output as HTML. Maybe you expected it, or maybe you did not; but we need to get to the root of this behavior.

The browser interpreted the output as HTML and rendered it accordingly, because the default value of the `Content-Type` header in Express is `text/html`.

However, we wanted the browser to treat the output as plain text and not bother rendering it as HTML.

Is there a way to enforce that behavior? Yes, there is a way. Using our newfound knowledge of HTTP headers and Express' `res.set()` method, we can set the `Content-Type` header to `text/plain`.

Update the code accordingly to confirm our assumption:

```
app.get('/', function(req, res) {
  res.set('Content-Type', 'text/plain');
  res.send('<h1>welcome</h1>');
});
```

Restart the app and reload the home page:

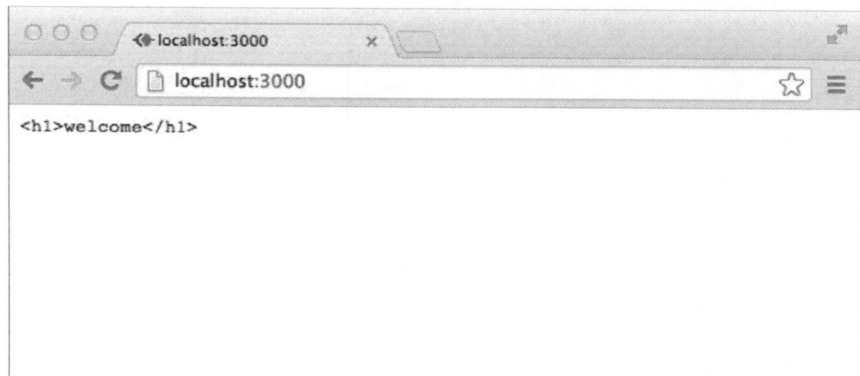

This time the content was really treated as plain text, like how we wanted. When the `Content-Type` is set to `text/plain`, the browser will render the body as plain text—this is the case even for binary files.

> The results of manually setting the `Content-Type` header for binary files may vary from browser to browser depending on many factors.

Although the exercise was about sending plain text data, we had a very good demonstration about the power of HTTP headers, especially the `Content-Type` header.

HTML

Being an HTTP server, sending the content as HTML is the default behavior of Express. Anything you send via `res.send()` or `res.render()` is sent as HTML by setting the `Content-Type` header to `text/html`.

As seen in a previous example, the following response body will be interpreted and rendered as HTML by the browser:

```
app.get('/', function(req, res) {
  res.send('<h1>welcome</h1>');
});
```

And in this example, Express will render a view using the Jade template engine, and generate a corresponding HTML page:

```
app.use(express.static('./public'));
app.set('views', __dirname + '/views');
app.set('view engine', 'jade');

app.get('/', function(req, res) {
  res.render('index', {title:'Express'});
});
```

If you look at the source code of the HTML code generated by Jade, you will find that the whole HTML is in a single line, as shown in the following screenshot:

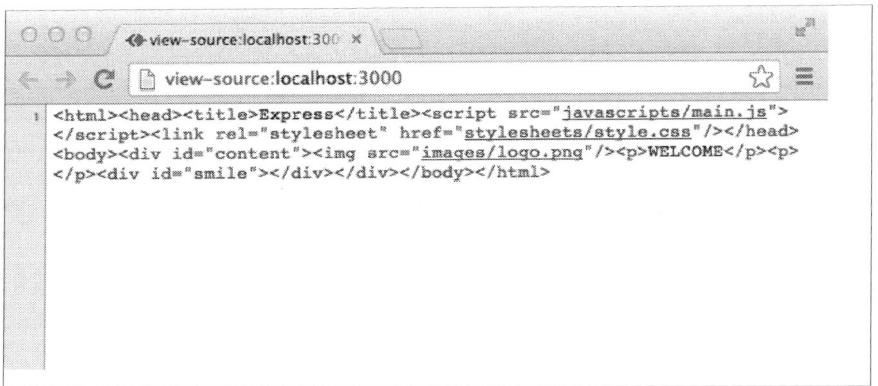

For whatever reason, you may sometimes want the HTML to be pretty-printed—show tags in separate lines with appropriate indentation to show hierarchy. To enable that, just set the value of `app.locals.pretty` in your app to `true`.

The previous code can be re-written as follows to prettify the generated HTML:

```
app.use(express.static('./public'));
app.set('views', __dirname + '/views');
app.set('view engine', 'jade');
```

```
// HTML should be prettified
app.locals.pretty = true;

app.get('/', function(req, res) {
  res.render('index', {title:'Express'});
});
```

Restart the server, reload the home page, and look at the source code now:

```
view-source:localhost:3000

<html>
  <head>
    <title>Express</title>
    <script src="javascripts/main.js"></script>
    <link rel="stylesheet" href="stylesheets/style.css"/>
  </head>
  <body>
    <div id="content"><img src="images/logo.png"/>
      <p>WELCOME</p>
      <p></p>
      <div id="smile"></div>
    </div>
  </body>
</html>
```

The generated HTML will now be pretty-printed. However, in a production environment it is best not to prettify HTML to save some processing power and reduce the download size of the HTML page.

JSON

Express provides the `res.json()` method for serving JSON content. You just have to pass an object to it, and it will take care of setting the up right headers and formatting the JSON string according to the JSON specifications.

Create this route for the home page:

```
app.get('/', function(req, res) {
  res.json({message: 'welcome'});
});
```

Start the app, load the home page, and examine the HTTP response headers:

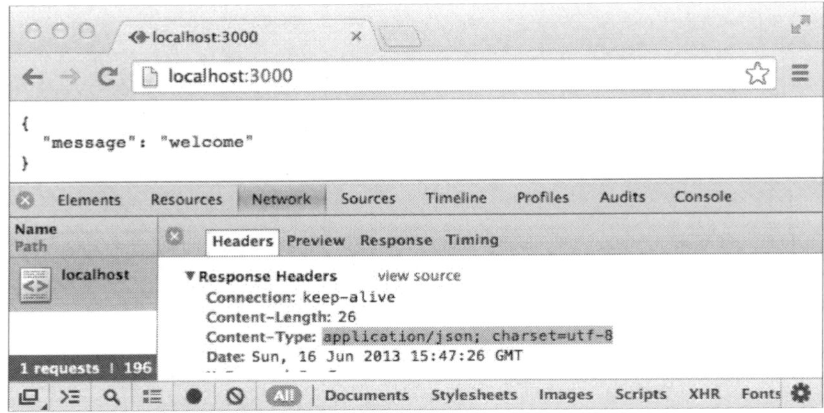

`res.json()` has successfully transformed the JavaScript object to a valid JSON string and set the appropriate HTTP headers for the message.

Like other response methods, `res.json()` sets a default of 200 when no status code is explicitly set. You can customize the status code by passing a number as the first parameter of `res.json()`, followed by the object to be sent:

```
res.json(404, {error: 'not found'});
```

Unlike `res.send()`, if you pass just a number to `res.json()`, it will be interpreted as the intended JSON object, and the default status code of 200 will be sent instead of using it as the status code.

JSONP

JSON with Padding (JSONP) is a JavaScript technique to allow cross-domain scripts to execute callbacks from JSON requests made to an external domain. It is beyond the scope of this book to cover JSONP in detail, but you can read it up at `http://en.wikipedia.org/wiki/JSONP`.

A JSONP request comes with a `GET` request parameter, conventionally named **callback**, which is the callback function available at the website making the request, which will be executed by passing the JSON result from the external domain.

JSONP requests to Express are handled by the `res.jsonp()` method. This method works like `res.json()`, except it wraps the JSON result with the callback function specified in the request.

Let's define the route of the home page to respond with `res.jsonp()`:

```
app.get('/', function(req, res) {
  res.jsonp({message: 'welcome'});
});
```

Start the server, load `http://localhost:3000/?callback=json_callback` in your browser, and examine the result:

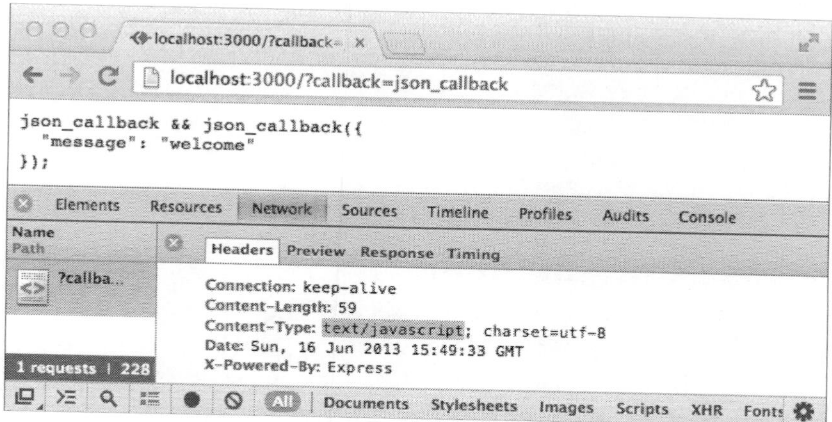

Not only did `res.jsonp()` wrap the JSON result with the callback function, it also added a quick check for the existence of the callback on the client machine before executing the callback. Also, it set the **Content-Type** header to the appropriate `text/javascript` content type so that the browser interprets the result as JavaScript.

By default, `res.jsonp()` expects the name of the callback parameter to be named `callback`, but it can be renamed to anything you like using the `app.set()` method, as shown here:

```
app.set('jsonp callback name', 'cb');
```

Now the callback name will be expected to be found in the `GET` parameter named `cb`. If the callback name is not found in the expected `GET` parameter, only the JSON object will be sent, without the callback padding.

Serving static files

As we saw in *Chapter 2, Your First Express App*, serving static files is very easy in Express—just set up a static directory using the static middleware and place the files there.

Create a directory named `files` in the app directory, keep the files in the directory, and add the following to the app file:

```
// Use the static middleware to set up a static files directory
app.use(express.static('./files'));
```

Now you can access all the files in the directory from the root of the website. This is how static files for the app, such as CSS, JavaScript, and image files are served in Express.

If you have a file named `logo.png` in the `files` directory, you can access it at `http://localhost:3000/logo.png`. Any file or subdirectory you create in the `files` directory will also be correspondingly accessible from the app, for example, `http://localhost:3000/new-logo.png`, `http://localhost:3000/icons/packt.png`, and so on.

Serving files programmatically

There is another category of files that can be served by a web server—those that are served dynamically—the requests to which you can apply programming logic.

Express provides two methods of handling such requests: `res.sendfile()` and `res.download()`. Let's examine them one after another.

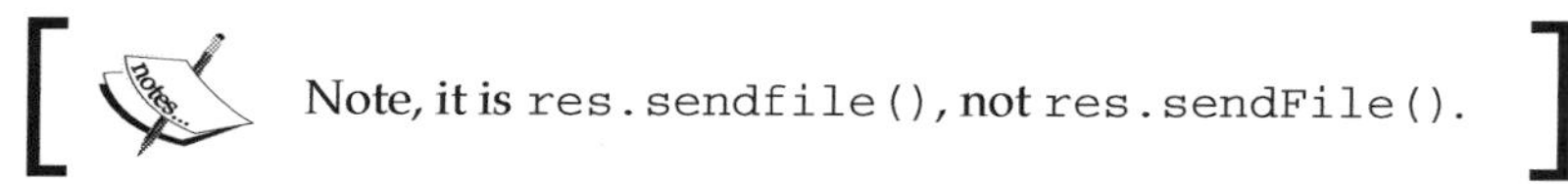

Note, it is `res.sendfile()`, not `res.sendFile()`.

Using `res.sendfile()`, you can send files to the browser in the same manner as how regular files are sent to it. The `Content-Type` header is automatically set based on the file extension, and depending on the file type and browser settings, the file may be shown in the browser, displayed by a plugin, prompted for download, and so on.

The following is a very simple example of using `res.sendfile()`:

```
app.get('/file', function(req, res) {
  res.sendfile('./secret-file.png', function(err) {
    if (err) { condole.log(err); }
    else { console.log('file sent'); }
  });
});
```

In this example, we send a private file from a private directory, to `GET` requests to the path/ file on the server.

In a web server context, public files and directories can be accessed via a URL, whereas private files and directories are those that are not exposed to the general public via a URL.

On loading `http://localhost:3000/file`, and examining the HTTP headers, we will find that no information about the actual name or location of the file was sent to the browser:

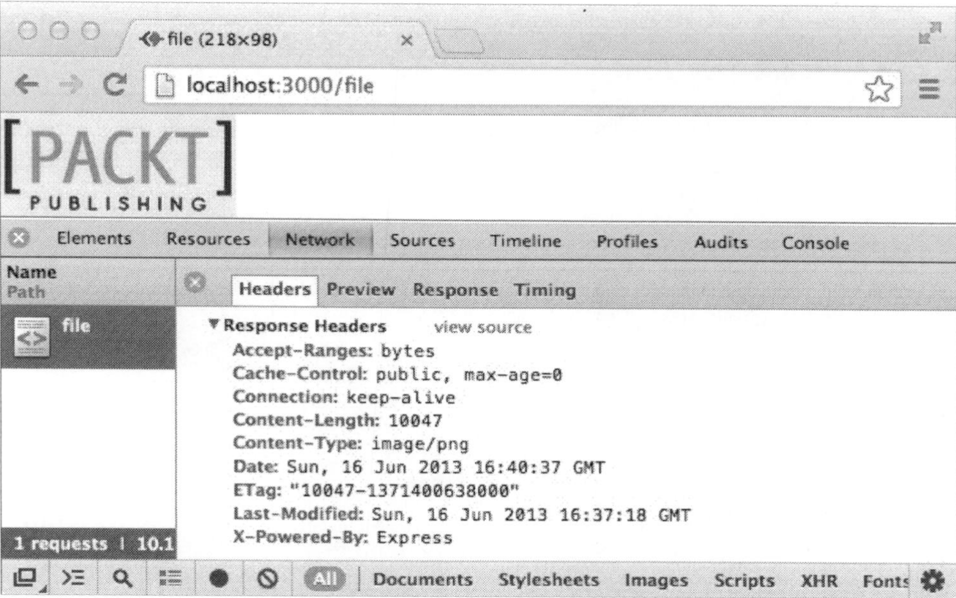

Considering the fact that routes names are very flexible and configurable in Express, you can do all sorts of useful or crazy things, when combined with `res.sendfile()`.

Here is an example that belongs to the crazy category:

```
app.get('/file.html', function(req, res) {
  console.log('HTML file is an image?');
  res.sendfile('./secret-file.png');
});
```

There are times when you want the user to actually download the file, and not let the browser try to render it. This can be achieved using the `res.download()` method.

`res.download()` requires the target file path, and accepts the optional desired filename and callback function for the download:

```
app.get('/download', function(req, res) {
  res.download('./secret-file.png', 'open-secret.png', function(err) {
    if (err) { condole.log(err); }
    else { console.log('file downloaded'); }
  });
});
```

If you examine the HTTP headers for this response, you will find that the **Content-Disposition** header has been set to attachment, because of which the file is being prompted for download or being downloaded:

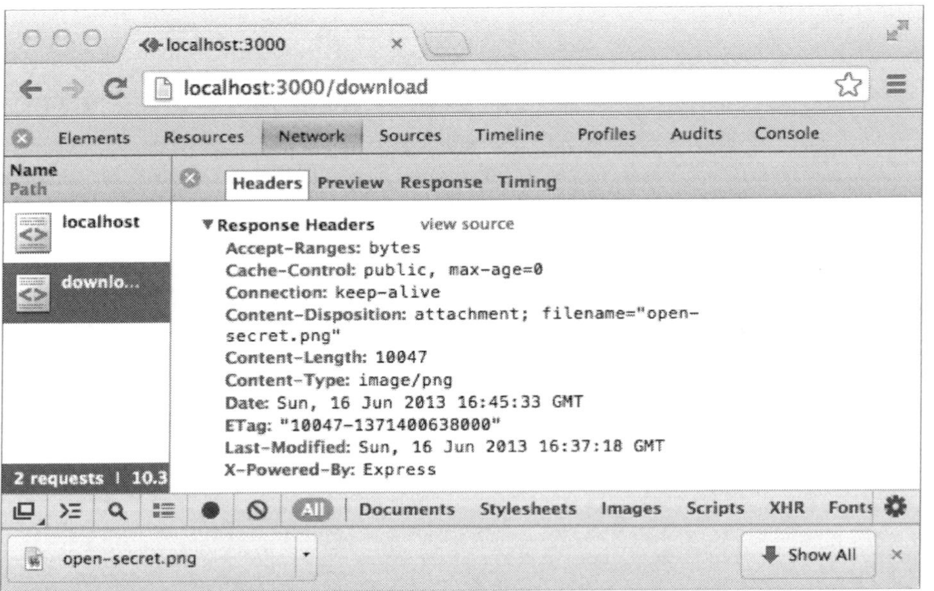

If a filename is not specified for the download to `res.download()`, the original name of the file will be used.

Serving error pages

Displaying an error page can be as simple as sending just an error status code with no body, or rendering an elaborate 404 or 500 error page.

The simplest way to display an error page is to just send the HTTP error code. In this case, the browser will "know" about the error, but the user will see just a blank screen.

```
// 404 error
res.send(404);
```

You can elaborate this a little bit more by adding a body that will be displayed in the browser. Now even the user will be aware about the error:

```
// 404 with additional message body
res.send(404, 'File not Found');
```

Using `res.render()`, you can have beautifully customized error pages for your website, if you want to.

In theory, using `res.send()` and `res.render()` to serve error pages sounds very straightforward and easy, however, in reality handling 404 and 500 errors is not that obvious to most beginners. Let's find out how we can catch these errors and send the appropriate responses.

We will be using views in the upcoming examples, so make sure you have set the `views` directory in the `app.js` file, or else the examples will fail to work. Refer *Chapter 2, Your First Express App*, for setting up views for your app.

The `router` middleware comes with a default 404 error handler, but its output may not be what you would want for your app. Let's find out how to create a custom 404 error handler.

A 404 error handler is technically a generic route handler that handles a request that all other middleware before it has failed to handle. It is implemented by adding a custom middleware at the end of the Express middleware stack.

Add the following middleware code after the `router` middleware:

```
app.use(function(req, res) {
  res.status(400);
  res.render('404.jade',
    {
      title: '404',
      message: 'File Not Found'
    }
  );
});
```

When the in-built 404 error handler detects that there is a route handler even beyond it, it will pass on the request to the next handler, which would be our custom 404 error handler.

In the `views` directory, create a file named `404.jade` with the following content:

```
doctype 5
html
  head
    title #{title}
  body
    h1 #{title}
    p #{message}
```

Restart the server and load a non-existent URL to see the 404 error page:

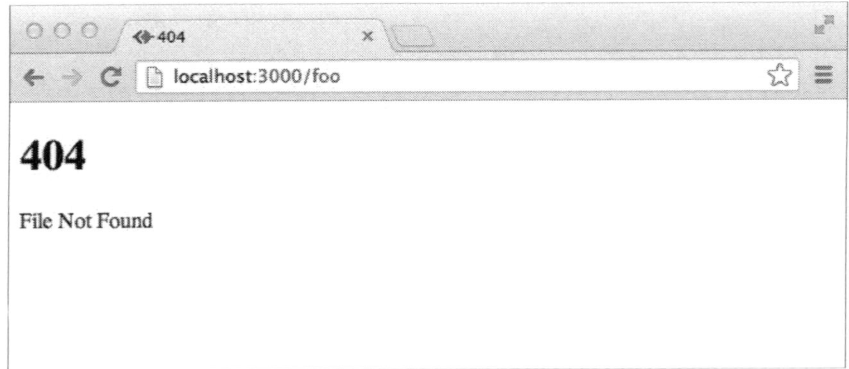

There you have it, your custom 404 error page! Feel free to modify and `customize404.jade` to your maximum satisfaction.

Express also comes with a default 500 error handler that will pass on the control to the next error handler, if there is one beyond it.

The 500 error is handled by adding a middleware with an arity of four. Since we want to override the default 500 error handler provided by the `router` middleware, we would need to add our handler after the `router` middleware.

Add the following middleware after the `router` middleware:

```
app.use(function(error, req, res, next) {
  res.status(500);
  res.render('500.jade',
```

```
      {
        title: '500',
        error: error
      }
    );
  });
```

Now create the corresponding `500.jade` view file in the `views` directory:

```
doctype 5
html
  head
    title #{title}
  body
    h1 #{title}
    p #{error}
```

To intentionally cause a 500 error, create a route with a callback that tries to execute an undefined function:

```
app.get('/error', function(req, res) {
  // Call an undefined function
  error();
});
```

Restart the app, load `http://localhost:3000/error` in your browser to see the 500 error page:

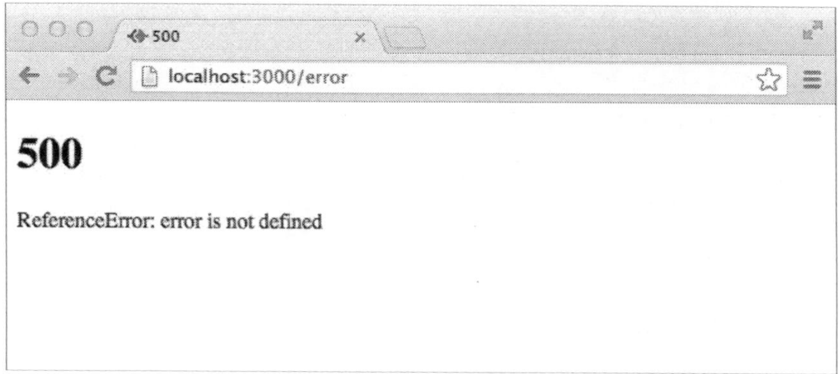

There you go, your own custom 500 error page!

Content negotiation

Content negotiation is the mechanism of specifying the data types a user agent is capable of consuming and prefers, and the server fulfilling the request when it can, and informing when it cannot.

User agents send their preferred content type for a resource using the `Accept` HTTP request header.

Express supports content negotiation using the `res.format()` method. This is a useful feature if you want to send different types of content based on the capability of the user agent.

`res.format()` accepts an object whose keys are the canonical content type name (`text/plain`, `text/html`, and so on), and whose values are functions that will be used as the handler for the route, for the matching content type.

Let's implement content negotiation in the home page route handler to find out how it works:

```
app.get('/', function(req, res) {

  res.format({

    'text/plain': function() {
      res.send('welcome');
    },

    'text/html': function() {
      res.send('<b>welcome</b>');
    },

    'application/json': function() {
      res.json({ message: 'welcome' });
    },

    'default': function() {
      res.send(406, 'Not Acceptable');
    }
  });

});
```

The server will respond with the appropriate data type based on the `Accept` header. This fact can be verified by sending an `Accept` header of `text/sgml, application/json`:

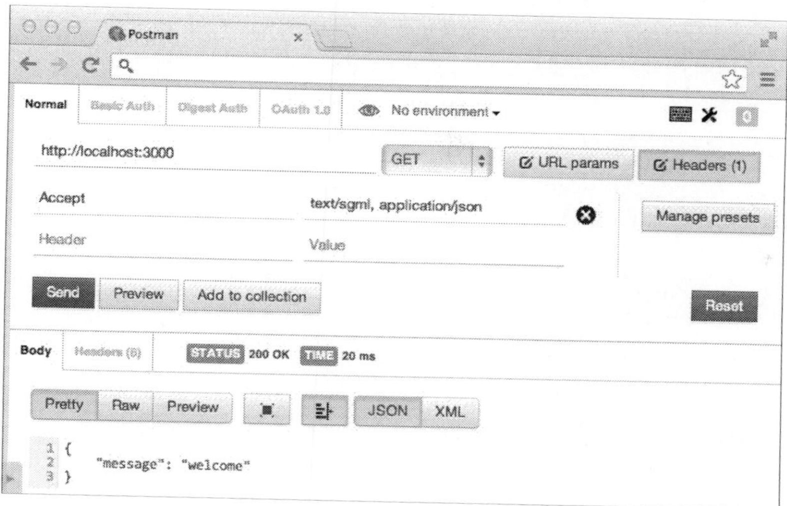

Similarly, you will get the corresponding content type if you set the `Accept` header to `text/plain` or `text/html`.

If a user agent does not support any of the specified formats in the handler, the server will return a status of **406 Not Acceptable**.

The previous code can be re-written in a less verbose manner by using just the subtype of the content type as the key:

```
res.format({

  text: function() {
    res.send('welcome');
  },

  html: function() {
    res.send('<b>welcome</b>');
  },

  json: function() {
    res.json({ message: 'welcome' });
  },

  default: function() {
    res.send(406, 'Not Acceptable');
  }
});
```

The `default` handler is optional. When not defined, an unsuccessful content negotiation will be handled by Express' built-in implementation of 406.

Redirecting a request

Sometimes you may want to redirect the request to a different URL, instead of responding with data. This is made possible in Express using the `res.redirect()` method. This method takes an optional redirection code that defaults to 302, and the URL to redirect to. The `URL` parameter can be an absolute URL or relative to the current URL.

The following are some examples of redirecting requests from an Express app:

Code	Description
`res.redirect('/notice');`	302 redirection to /`notice` relative to the requested URL
`res.redirect(301, '/help-docs');`	301 redirection to /`help-docs` relative to the requested URL
`res.redirect('http://nodejs.org/api/');`	301 redirection to an absolute URL
`res.redirect('../images');`	302 redirection to /`notice` relative to the requested URL

Summary

We now know that a lot more happens in the background when we load something in the browser. We learned to customize the HTTP response object in Express to control the outcome of the request and serve different content types from our app.

We were introduced to Jade in *Chapter 2, Your First Express App*, and it has been a constant presence in all the chapters till now. So far we know that it is a templating engine and works great for generating HTML from our app. There is much more to Jade than what we saw in the examples, in the next chapter we will learn about it in greater detail.

5
The Jade Templating Language

Jade is the recommended template engine for Express. It comes with an intuitive language to create templates and views for Express apps. Jade, the template engine has many aspects to it, but in this chapter we will focus only on its templating capabilities.

You will learn the following in this chapter:

- How to create HTML tags using Jade
- How to use filters such as Markdown with Jade
- How to modularize views
- How to use the programming capabilities of Jade

What is Jade?

Jade, the templating language has a very intuitive syntax. You will most likely understand 70 percent of how Jade works just by looking at an example. In fact, the best way to start learning Jade is to look at a moderately complex Jade example and try to make sense of it.

In this chapter, we will be focusing only on the language aspect of Jade. For other details about Jade, visit the official Jade website at `http://jade-lang.com/`.

Jade support is not enabled in Express apps by default. Jade is one of the many template engines supported by Express. We will need to configure our app to support Jade by setting two app variables: one for setting the view engine to jade, and the other to set the `views` directory, where the view files for the app will be located:

```
app.set('view engine', 'jade');
app.set('views','./views');
```

Let's set up a quick app to see an example of Jade code in action.

The following is the content for `app.js`. Note that we have specified that a view named `index` should be rendered for `GET` requests to the home page:

```
var express = require('express');
var http = require('http');
var app = express();

app.set('view engine', 'jade');
app.set('views','./views');

app.use(app.router);
app.use(express.static('./public'));
app.locals.pretty = true;

app.get('/', function(req, res) {
  res.render('index', {title:'Learning Jade'});
});

http.createServer(app).listen(3000, function(){
  console.log('App started');
});
```

Create a file named `index.jade` in the `views` directory with the following content:

```
doctype 5
html

  head
    title #{title}
    style(type='text/css')
      #wrapper {
        font: 14px Arial;
        width: 300px;
        padding: 5px;
        border: 1px solid #ccc;
```

```
          margin: 0 auto;
        }
        #content {
          margin: 10px 0;
        }
        .highlighted {
          background: #d0ff5e;
        }

  body
    #wrapper

      h1 #{title}
      #content
        p Jade is intuitive, Jade is logical. Jade makes HTML easy,
Jade saves time.
        p.highlighted Here is some highlighted text.
        button#alert Click Me

      footer
        span Copyright &copy; 2013
        a(href='/') Home

    // script tag at the end to query the DOM straightaway
    script
      var greeting = 'Welcome to Jade';
      document.querySelector('#alert').onclick = function() {
        alert(greeting);
      };
```

Start the app and load the home page. On viewing the source of the page, you will find the following HTML:

```
<!DOCTYPE html>
<html>
<head>
<title>Learning Jade</title>
<style type="text/css">
      #wrapper {
        font: 14px Arial;
        width: 300px;
        padding: 5px;
        border: 1px solid #ccc;
        margin: 0 auto;
      }
```

```
        #content {
          margin: 10px 0;
        }
        .highlighted {
          background: #d0ff5e;
        }

  </style>
  </head>
  <body>
  <div id="wrapper">
  <h1>Learning Jade</h1>
  <div id="content">
  <p>Jade is intuitive, Jade is logical. Jade makes HTML easy, Jade
  saves time.</p>
  <p class="highlighted">Here is some highlighted text.</p>
  <button id="alert">Click Me</button>
  </div>
  <footer><span>Copyright &copy; 2013 </span><a href="/">Home</a></
  footer>
  </div>
  <!-- script tag at the end to query the DOM straightaway-->
  <script>
        var greeting = 'Welcome to Jade';
        document.querySelector('#alert').onclick = function() {
          alert(greeting);
        };
  </script>
  </body>
  </html>
```

Try to correlate the Jade code and the HTML output. Pay good attention to the indentation. This exercise will prepare you for learning more about Jade in the upcoming sections.

Anytime you make some change in a view file, it will be reflected immediately, without having to restart the server. Just refresh the page to see the change.

Generating HTML tags

HTML tags are created by the mere mention of their names in the view file. If you would like to include any text within a tag, include it right after the tag name.

The way tags work in Jade is best understood by looking at these examples:

Jade	HTML
html	<html></html>
div	<div></div>
div Hello World!	<div>Hello World!</div>
br	
script	<script></script>
span Howdy?	<span>Howdy?</span>

It is important to note that it is your responsibility to use valid HTML tag names, Jade will just create an element—valid or not.

Hierarchy of HTML elements

In HTML, we create hierarchical DOM elements by nesting elements within other elements with the use of opening and closing tags. In Jade, we create hierarchy by the use of indentations—a tag indented below a tag is hierarchically placed under the former tag.

You can use either tabs or spaces for indentation. Whichever you choose, stick to one; mixing both will cause Jade to throw an error.

Let's look at some examples to see how indentations in Jade work to create hierarchy in the HTML output:

Jade	HTML
div span	<div> <span></span> </div>
div span Hola!	<div> <span>Hola!</span> </div>

div
  div
    button Click Me
	<div>
	<div>
	<button>Click Me</button>
	</div>
	</div>

Jade	HTML

html
  head
    title Hello
  body Hello World!
	<html>
	<head>
	<title>Hello</title>
	</head>
	<body>Hello World!</body>
	</html>

Sometimes, the number of indentations can get too nested. In the case of tags without text, you can use Jade's block expansion feature to define the hierarchy on one line. The block expansion uses a colon after the tag.

Here are some examples to show you how block expansions work:

Jade	HTML
div: a(href='/about') About Me	<div> <a href="/about">About Me</a> </div>
div: ul: li One	<div> <ul> <li>One</li> </ul> </div>
div.container: div.content Hello!	<div class="container"> <div class="content">Hello!</div> </div>
div.one: div.two: div.three Three levels deep	<div class="one"> <div class="two"> <div class="three">Three levels deep</div> </div> </div>
div: span: strong: em: #main	<div> <span> <strong> <em> <div id="main"></div> </em> </strong> </span> </div>

Block expansion works best when there are no text nodes within the involved tags, the only exception being the last tag.

Assigning IDs

An ID can be assigned to a tag by using the ID marker (#). If the ID marker is used without any tag name, the tag is assumed to be div tag.

Here are some examples to help you understand how ID assignment works in Jade:

Jade	HTML
p#main-content	<p id="main-content"></p>
span#target	<span id="target"></span>
div#username DiamondDave	<div id="username">DiamondDave</ div>

#social
  #fb Facebook
  #twitter Twitter
	<div id="social">
	<div id="fb">Facebook</div>
	<div id="twitter">Twitter</div>
	</div>

Since an ID is an HTML element's attribute, it can also be assigned to a tag using the attribute assignment feature, which is covered in an upcoming section.

If you haven't noticed already, Jade's ID marker is derived from the CSS ID selector.

Assigning classes

Like the ID marker, Jade uses the CSS class selector to mark classes. A tag can be assigned a class by using the class marker (.). Multiple classes can be assigned to a tag. If the class marker is used without a tag, it is assumed to be a div tag.

Let's look at some examples:

Jade	HTML
.highlighted This text is highlighted	<div class="highlighted">This text is highlighted</div>
#target.highlighted ID and class together	<div id="target" class="highlighted">ID and class together</div>
.highlighted#target Order doesn't matter	<div id="target" class="highlighted">Order doesn't matter</div>
.highlighted.important Multiple classes	<div class="highlighted important">Multiple classes</div>
p.normal .start The text starts here	<p class="normal"> <div class="start">The text starts here</div> </p>

Specifying HTML attributes

The ID and class markers were used to set the `id` and `class` attributes of tags. But we can't afford a symbol for all the possible attributes of HTML tags. This problem is addressed by the use of a generic attribute operator to assign attributes to a tag.

The attribute operator consists of an opening and a closing parenthesis, with the arguments and their values enclosed within them. The following examples will give you a good idea about how attributes are created in Jade:

Jade	HTML
p(id='main', class='highlight special')	<p id="main" class="highlight special"></p>
#main(data-name='Lee')	<div id="main" data-name="Dave"></div>
a(href='/main').special#main-link	<a href="/main" id="main-link" class="special"></a>
img(src='/images/logo.png')#logo.	<img src="/images/logo.png" id="logo"/>

You can set the value of an attribute using a variable by referring to it without the quotes. Variables in Jade are covered a little later:

Jade	HTML
`- user_type = 'regular'` `div(class=user_type) Hi`	`<div class="regular">Hi</div>`

Creating text content

As seen in some of the examples, adding text to a tag is just about putting it right after a tag:

Jade	HTML
`div Here goes some text`	`<div>Here goes some text</div>`
`p One-line paragraph`	`<p>One-line paragraph</p>`
`button Click Me`	`<button>Click Me</button>`

The preceding method works very well for single-line text, but it cannot handle multiline text. So how do we write multiline text?

There are two ways of handling this: text blocks defined using the bar notation and the dot notation.

The bar notation uses the vertical bar character (|) to mark the contents of a text block. The text block should be indented within the containing tag:

Jade

```
p
  | one two
  | buckle my shoe

pre
  | step 1
  |   step 2
  |     step 3
```

HTML

```
<p>
  one two
  buckle my shoe
</p>
<pre>step 1
  step 2
    step 3</pre>
```

Text blocks can also be used seamlessly with other nested elements, as shown in the following examples:

Jade

```
p
  | Username:
  span.username DiamondDave
```

HTML

```
<p>Username: <span
class="username">DiamondDave</
span></p>
```

Jade	HTML

`p`
  `span Diamond`
  `span Dave`
  `| is the`
  `span  username`
	`<p>`
	`<span>Diamond</span>`
	`<span>Dave</span>is the`
	`<span> username</span>`
	`</p>`

The bar notation works fine for a few lines of text, especially with other nested elements, but it becomes awkward when dealing with large contiguous chunks of text.

The dot notation uses a suffixed dot to mark the text block to be contained within a tag. Note that there should be no space between the tag and the dot, or else it will be interpreted as a literal dot:

Jade	HTML

`p.`
  `one two`
  `buckle my shoe`
	`<p>`
	  `one two`
	  `buckle my shoe`
	`</p>`

`pre.`
  `step 1`
    `step 2`
      `step 3`
	`<pre>step 1`
	  `step 2`
	    `step 3</pre>`
	`<p>`

The dot notation works best with large chunks of contiguous text.

For `style` and `script` tags, you don't need define text blocks. You can indent the appropriate content and they will be rendered accordingly, as shown in the following examples:

Jade	HTML

`style`
  `body {`
    `padding: 10px;`
    `font: 14px Arial;`
  `}`
	`<style>`
	  `body {`
	    `padding: 10px;`
	    `font: 14px Arial;`
	  `}`
	`</style>`

`script`
  `var name = 'Dave';`
  `alert(name);`
	`<script>`
	  `var name = 'Dave';`
	  `alert(name);`
	`</script>`

Filters

The default text blocks in Jade work well for simple text segments, but can become problematic for large segments with lots of formatting. That's where text-to-HTML filters such as Markdown excel.

Filters are Jade's way of supporting other text formatters within it. Jade is currently compatible with Stylus, Less, Markdown, CDATA, and CoffeeScript. Filter blocks are marked by a colon, followed by the name of the filter.

Filters for Stylus, Less, Markdown, CDATA, and CoffeeScript, don't work right out of the box; you will need to install their respective packages for the filters to work in your code.

Let's find out how filters work using Markdown as an example.

First, install the `markdown` Node package by executing the following command:

```
$ npm install markdown
```

With the package installed, you will be able to use Markdown in your code. The following is an example of using the Markdown syntax within the Markdown filter in a Jade view:

```
#content

  :markdown

    #Websites

    1. [Wikipedia](http://www.wikipedia.org/)
    2. [Google](http://www.google.com/)
    3. [Yahoo!](http://www.yahoo.com/)

    **IMPORTANT**: Install the 'markdown' module
```

The preceding Jade code will output the following HTML code:

```
<div id="content">
<h2>Websites</h2>
<ol>
<li><a href="http://www.wikipedia.org/">Wikipedia</a></li>
<li><a href="http://www.google.com/">Google</a>
</li><li><a href="http://www.yahoo.com/">Yahoo!</a></li>
</ol>
<p>
```

```
<strong>IMPORTANT</strong>: Install the <code>markdown</code> module
</p>
</div>
```

If you were to accomplish the same thing using Jade, it would have been a lot more tedious. For large chunks of text with no dynamic content, it's advisable to use filters to save time.

Local variables in views can be accessed from filter blocks but their behavior is not optimal at the moment, so don't rely on it.

Declaring the document's Doctype

The Doctype of the document is declared by using the `doctype` keyword followed by an optional Doctype value. If no value is specified, it defaults to `html`. Alternatively, you can use `!!!` instead of `doctype`.

The following table lists the predefined values of Doctype:

Jade	HTML
`doctype`	`<!DOCTYPE html>`
`doctype 5`	`<!DOCTYPE html>`
`doctype default`	`<!DOCTYPE html>`
`doctype transitional`	`<!DOCTYPE html PUBLIC "-//W3C//DTD XHTML 1.0 Transitional//EN" "http://www.w3.org/TR/xhtml1/DTD/xhtml1-transitional.dtd">`
`doctype strict`	`<!DOCTYPE html PUBLIC "-//W3C//DTD XHTML 1.0 Strict//EN" "http://www.w3.org/TR/xhtml1/DTD/xhtml1-strict.dtd">`
`doctype frameset`	`<!DOCTYPE html PUBLIC "-//W3C//DTD XHTML 1.0 Frameset//EN" "http://www.w3.org/TR/xhtml1/DTD/xhtml1-frameset.dtd">`
`doctype 1.1`	`<!DOCTYPE html PUBLIC "-//W3C//DTD XHTML 1.1//EN" "http://www.w3.org/TR/xhtml11/DTD/xhtml11.dtd">`
`doctype basic`	`<!DOCTYPE html PUBLIC "-//W3C//DTD XHTML Basic 1.1//EN" "http://www.w3.org/TR/xhtml-basic/xhtml-basic11.dtd">`

Jade	HTML
`doctype mobile`	`<!DOCTYPE html PUBLIC "-//WAPFORUM//DTD XHTML Mobile 1.2//EN" "http://www.openmobilealliance.org/tech/DTD/xhtml-mobile12.dtd">`
`doctype xml`	`<?xml version="1.0" encoding="utf-8" ?>`

Apart from the predefined Doctypes, you can pass a literal and declare any Doctype you want to. The probability of you using this method is very slim, but in case you need to, here are some examples to follow:

Jade	HTML
`doctype html PUBLIC "-//W3C//DTD XHTML Basic 1.1//EN"`	`<!DOCTYPE html public "-//w3c//dtd xhtml basic 1.1//en">`
`doctype html DIY "-//WHATEVER"`	`<!DOCTYPE html diy "-//whatever">`
`doctype my-custom-doctype`	`<!DOCTYPE my-custom-doctype>`

Programmability in Jade

Jade is not just about static tags and contents. Especially being a templating language, it is expected of Jade to support variables, interpolation, and various programming capabilities.

In this section, we will explore the various programmable aspects of Jade.

Even though Jade provides programming capability, it is primarily a template engine; hence it is recommended to minimize programming in the view files.

Variables

Variables in a Jade file can come from the `app.locals` object, the `res.locals` object, the `res.render()` method, or can be defined right in the view file.

Any variable defined in the `app.globals` object will be available to all the views of the app. Variables defined in the `app.res.globals` object will be available to the view rendering the response.

Variables from `res.render()` are passed to a Jade template as the second parameter of `res.render()`, as key-value pairs of an object.

In the very first example of this chapter, we had a route handler that passed the `title` variable to its view:

```
app.get('/', function(req, res) {
  res.render('index', {title:'Learning Jade'});
});
```

We used the `title` variable for setting the title of the page and the main header:

```
title #{title}
...
h1 #{title}
```

To add more variables in the view, we just add more properties on the object that will be passed to the renderer:

```
app.get('/', function(req, res) {
  res.render('index', {
    title: 'Superheroes',
    message: 'The champs are back!',
    html_message: 'The <b>champs</b> are back!'
  });
});
```

In this example, three variables: `title`, `message`, and `html_message` will be available to the `index` view.

Although the most common way of creating variables in a view is to pass them through the `res.render()` method, we can declare variables right in the view file too. There are two ways of declaring variables in a view file: using plain JavaScript and using the Jade construct for variable declaration.

> Jade constructs are designer-friendly wrappers on the top of actual JavaScript constructs. They provide a less verbose and a "friendlier" interface to various programming constructs available in JavaScript. You will get to see more of them in the upcoming sections.

The JavaScript way of declaring a variable is to start a line with a hyphen (`-`), and follow with the regular JavaScript statement of variable declaration. The ending semicolon is optional:

```
- var title = 'Super!'
```

The Jade way of declaring is a lot like JavaScript, except you don't have to start with a hyphen or use the `var` keyword:

```
title = 'Super!'
```

Note that, whether a variable came from the route handler or was defined in the view, it always refers to the same instance. If you are not careful, you can end up overwriting a variable passed by the router handler, in the view.

We learned that defining the `pretty` variable in the view is supposed to prettify HTML; however, if you define it in the view file it will not work as expected. It works only if it is defined in `app.locals`, `res.locals`, or came from `res.render()`. That is because its value is required before the view is rendered.

Interpolation

Now that we know how variables are created in views, let's find out how to use them and render their values in the generated HTML.

There are two main types of interpolations available in Jade: placeholders and expressions. Each of these types has an escaped and an unescaped version:

Interpolation	Escaped	Unescaped
Placeholder	`#{variable}`	`!{variable}`
Expression	`= variable`	`!= variable`

Escaped interpolation will escape any HTML code in the variable to display is actual characters in the rendered HTML, instead of formatting them. Unescaped interpolation will result in rendering of the HTML if the variable contains any.

Be very careful about using the unescaped version of interpolation or your app will be susceptible to XSS attacks. Read more about XSS at `https://www.owasp.org/index.php/Cross-site_Scripting_%28XSS%29`.

In placeholder interpolation, variables are rendered by enclosing them within the braces of `#{}` or `!{}`, depending on your requirement. The only exception is values of HTML attributes; they are interpreted without the evaluation enclosures:

Jade	HTML
p #{title} - #{html_message}	<p>Superheroes - The <b>champs</b> are back!</p>
p #{title} - !{html_message}	<p>Superheroes - The <b>champs</b> are back!</p>
img(alt=title, src='/logo.png')	<img alt="Superheroes" src="/logo.png">

You can notice that the HTML code is not rendered in the first example, because we used the escaped interpolation. In the unescaped example, the HTML code in the variable is rendered along with the Jade code.

Placeholders works very well for large chunks of text with variable sections within it. Here is an example:

```
actor_type = 'frog'
actor_name = 'Croaky'
territory = 'pond'
territory_name = 'Pondy'

p Once upon a time there was a #{actor_type} named #{actor_name}, in
a #{territory} called #{territory_name}. #{actor_name} was loved by
everyone in #{territory_name}.
```

The preceding Jade code will be rendered into the following HTML code:

```
<p>Once upon a time there was a frog named Croaky, in a pond called
Pondy. Croaky was loved by everyone in Pondy.</p>
```

Expression interpolation works best for displaying the contents of a single variable. You can use either the escaped (=) or the unescaped (!=) version, depending on your requirement:

Jade	HTML
p= title	<p>Superheroes</p>
p= html_message	<p>The <b>champs</b> are back!</p>
p!= html_message	<p>The <b>champs</b> are back!</p>

Since expression interpolation uses JavaScript expressions, it is not limited to displaying just a single variable. You can use the JavaScript concatenation operator (+) to string together multiple variables into a single expression and even include simple JavaScript expressions:

Jade	HTML
`p= '© ' + new Date().getFullYear()`	`<p>© 2013</p>`
`p= actor_name + ' is a ' + actor_type`	`<p>Croaky is a frog</p>`

Although expression interpolation can be used to string together multiple variables, it is best suited for rendering individual variables. Here is how it would look, if we were to rewrite Croaky's story using expression interpolation:

```
p= 'Once upon a time there was a ' + actor_type + ' named ' + actor_
name + ', in a ' + territory + ' called ' + territory_name +'. '+
actor_name + ' was loved by everyone in '+ territory_name + '.'
```

Not pretty at all, and definitely not the way templates should be used.

Another important difference between placeholders and expressions is that you can use expressions without any containing tag, but if you try the same with a placeholder, you will end up creating a tag with the value of the variable:

Jade	HTML
`= title`	`Superheroes`
`#{title}`	`<Superheroes></Superheroes>`

Control structures

Two types of control structures are available in Jade: JavaScript constructs and Jade constructs. As a JavaScript programmer, the former will be instantly familiar to you. The latter are custom implementations of various programming constructs, the syntax of which is a lot inspired by Python.

Let's define a route and its handler to base our examples:

```
app.get('/', function(req, res) {
  res.render('index', {
    title: 'Superheroes',
    heroes: [
      {name: 'Fooman', role: 'captain', skills: ['dancing',
'invisibility']},
```

```
        {name: 'Barman', role: 'entertainer', skills: ['bar tending',
'x-ray vision']},
        {name: 'Napman', role: 'hacker', skills: ['computer hacking',
'nunchucks']},
        {name: 'Zipman', role: 'collector', skills: ['zipping',
'flight']}
      ]
    });
  });
```

JavaScript constructs

JavaScript code works mostly as expected with some limitations and exceptions in a Jade view. The most important part is to start the line with a hyphen (-) to indicate that the following expression is in JavaScript.

Here is a JavaScript `for` loop in a view:

```
- for (var i in heroes) {
  div #{i}. #{heroes[i].name}
- }
```

The preceding code will generate the following HTML:

```
<div>0. Fooman</div>
<div>1. Barman</div>
<div>2. Napman</div>
<div>3. Zipman</div>
```

The same can be achieved using a slight modification—by omitting the braces. However, make sure you indent your code well. The tag code should be indented within the hyphen that marked the `for` loop:

```
- for (var i in heroes)
  div #{i}. #{heroes[i].name}
```

Here is another example to demonstrate the use of JavaScript conditionals in a view:

```
- if (typeof(title) != 'undefined')
  = title
- else
  = 'Title is missing'
```

Since the `title` variable is declared, Jade will print the value in the browser.

Here we demonstrate another JavaScript construct—the `forEach()` method:

```
- heroes.forEach(function(hero, i) {
```

```
    div= hero.name
  - })
```

Since we are passing a callback function to the method, we cannot omit the curly braces. The preceding code will generate the following HTML:

```
<div>Fooman</div>
<div>Barman</div>
<div>Napman</div>
<div>Zipman</div>
```

Most JavaScript constructs are valid programming constructs in a Jade view, and curly braces are optional in simple blocks.

In the following example, we use the JavaScript `while` loop to count from `10` to `1`:

```
pre

  n = 10
  - while (n > 0)
    = n + '\n'
    - n--
```

And this is how we define a function and call it:

```
- function greet(name)
  p Hi #{name}!

- greet('Fred')
- greet('Ned')
```

JavaScript code, especially with the leading hyphens, can start to look untidy and confusing if you use it a lot in your views. Try to avoid using JavaScript in your views; if you must, consider the neater Jade constructs.

The main purpose of view files is to generate HTML content. If you are applying any complex programming logic to the data in views, you should re-evaluate your implementation and hand over the responsibility to the controller or the route handler that passed the variable.

Jade constructs

Jade constructs are the designer-friendly implementation on top of the underlying JavaScript constructs—you use indentation to create code blocks, and you don't have to use hyphens, parentheses, and braces.

Jade constructs are currently limited to `if`, `else if`, `else`, `for`, `each`, `case`, `while`, and `unless`. Let's study them one by one, using some examples.

if, else if, and else

The `if`, `else if`, and `else` combination works just like in JavaScript, except you don't have to use parentheses and braces. Another important thing to note is that you indent the code within a conditional to execute it under that condition:

```
if hero.role == 'captain'
  .msg Aye Captain!
else if hero.role == 'hacker' && hero.name != 'Napman'
  .msg Who goes there?
else
  .msg Avast!
```

for

The `for` construct works like the JavaScript `for-in` loop:

```
for hero in heroes
  div= hero.name
```

In case you need to access the index:

```
for hero, i in heroes
  div Hero No.#{i} - #{hero.name}
```

You can access the properties of an object that is being iterated in a `for` loop, as expected:

```
for hero in heroes
  if hero.role == 'hacker'
    div Got the hacker!
    - break
  div= hero.role
```

each

The closest sounding construct to Jade's `each` construct, in JavaScript, is `forEach()`.

`each` and `for` are aliases to each other, you can substitute `for` in the preceding examples with `each` and will still get the same results.

The reason we have two constructs that do the same thing is because of developer preference—some of us feel at home with the `for` iteration, while some of us prefer to use `each`.

while

The `while` construct is a part of JavaScript's `while` loop:

```
i = 0

while i < 5
  div= i
  i++
```

unless

The `unless` construct is an alternative way to check for Boolean false.

Here is an example showing the use of the `unless` construct:

```
each hero in heroes
  unless hero.role == 'captain'
    div #{hero.name}, report for duty!
```

The preceding code does the same thing as the following:

```
each hero in heroes
  if hero.role != 'captain'
    div #{hero.name}, report for duty!
```

case

The `case` construct is Jade's less verbose and neater-looking implementation of the JavaScript `switch-case` construct:

```
case hero.role
  when 'captain'
    div Yarr!
when 'hacker'
    div w00t!
  default
    div Avast!
```

Modularization

In this section, we will go through the ways Jade views can be modularized at file and code level.

Includes

A Jade view file can seamlessly include other Jade files, CSS, JavaScript, and HTML files. If you have installed the `markdown` Node module, you can include Markdown files too.

To include a file in a view, use the `include` directive and pass it the path of the file to be included. It is very important to give the correct extension to the include files, because Jade uses the extension of the file to render the content accordingly.

A Jade view file and its included Jade files share the same scope. So variables defined in one file are available to the other.

The indented hierarchy is applicable to the `include` directive too, so the way you indent it is important.

Let's create an example to understand how `include` works. In the `views` directory of your app, create a new directory named `includes`, where we will be creating the following include files:

1. A Jade file named `header.jade` with the following content:

   ```
   h1 Included Header
   ```

2. A Markdown file named `content.md` with the following content:

   ```
   The Main Content
   ----------------
   A **Markdown** file was included and rendered in the HTML.
   ```

3. An HTML file named `footer.html` with the following content:

   ```
   <div id="footer">Footer &copy; 2013</div>
   ```

4. A CSS file named `style.css` with the following content:

   ```
   body {
     padding: 10px;
     font: 14px Arial, sans-serif;
   }
   a {
     color: #0066ff;
   }
   ```

5. A JavaScript file named `script.js` with the following content:

   ```
   alert('JavaScript included');
   ```

6. And then the view file (`index.jade`) that goes in the `views` directory, which will include the files in the `includes` directory:

```
!!! 5
html
  head
    title Include Examples
    include includes/style.css
  body
    include includes/header.jade
    include includes/content.md
 p ... and here is something original from the Jade file.
    include includes/footer.html
    include includes/script.js
```

When this view file is rendered, you will get the following HTML:

```
<!DOCTYPE html>
<html>
<head>
<title>Include Examples</title>
<style>body {
      font: 14px Arial;
      padding: 10px;
    }
</style>
</head>
<body>
<h1>Included Header</h1>
<h2>The Main Content</h2>
<p>A <strong>Markdown</strong> file was included and rendered in the
HTML.</p>
<p>... and here is something original from the Jade file.</p>
<div id="footer">Footer &copy; 2013</div>
<script>alert('JavaScript included');</script>
</body>
</html>
```

Template inheritance

If you have multiple views with a similar structure, you will end up with the same set of includes in all your views. This approach can quickly become complicated and untidy, if the number of views and includes increases.

Includes work best with small sets of sub-views, popularly called **partials**.

An alternative to `includes` is template inheritance. In this method we create templates with blocks in them, the contents of which are then filled in by the views extending the template.

Let's find out how templates work using some examples.

Create a template named `layout.jade` with the following content:

```
!!! 5
html
  head
    title Learning Inheritance
    link(rel='stylesheet', href='/stylesheets/style.css')
  body
p The inherited content goes below:
    block content
    block footer
```

We have defined two blocks named `content` and `footer` using the `block` directive. Views extending this template can define the contents for the blocks, if they wish too.

Let's create a view to extend the `layout` template, with the following content:

```
extends layout

block content
  h2 Image Content
  img(src='/images/01.jpg')

block footer
  #footer Images - Copyright &copy; 2013
```

We used the `extends` directive to indicate that this view is extending the `layout.jade` template. In the view, we defined the contents for the `content` and `footer` blocks that it inherited from the template.

Rendering this view will generate the following HTML:

```
<!DOCTYPE html>
<html>
<head>
<title>Learning Inheritance</title>
<link rel="stylesheet" href="/stylesheets/style.css">
</head>
<body>
<p>The inherited content goes below:</p>
<h2>Image Content</h2>
```

```
<img src="/images/01.jpg">
<div id="footer">Images - Copyright &copy; 2013</div>
</body>
</html>
```

Create another view, which extends `layout`, with the following content:

```
extends layout

block content
  h2 Text Content
  p.
    Jade is intuitive, Jade is logical.
Jade makes HTML easy, Jades saves time.

block footer
  #footer Text - Copyright &copy; 2013
```

On rendering this view, the following HTML will be generated:

```
<!DOCTYPE html>
<html>
<head>
<title>Learning Inheritance</title>
<link rel="stylesheet" href="/stylesheets/style.css">
</head>
<body>
<p>The inherited content goes below:</p>
<h2>Text Content</h2>
<p>
      Jade is intuitive, Jade is logical.
      Jade makes HTML easy, Jade saves time.
</p>
<div id="footer">Text - Copyright &copy; 2013</div>
</body>
</html>
```

From the preceding examples, we can see that the template defines the blocks, and the views extending the template define the content of those blocks.

Template inheritance is not just about replacing empty blocks. Blocks can have content of their own by default; those extending the template can then either replace it, prepend it, or append to it. Views that don't define the content of a block will inherit the content defined in the template, and will be rendered accordingly.

The default behavior of template inheritance is replacement, which was seen in the previous examples. To prepend a block, we use the `block prepend` directive, or just `prepend`. Similarly, to append a block, we use the `block append` directive, the shorter version of which is `append`.

The replacement, prepend, append, and default inheritance behaviors are demonstrated in the following example.

Here is the content of the template file, named `layout-demo.jade`:

```
!!! 5
html
  head
    block head
      script(src='/library.js')
  body
    block content
      p Default Content
    block footer
      #footer The original footer
```

And here is the content of the view, which extends it:

```
extend layout-demo

prepend head
  script(src='/one.js')

append head
  script(src='/two.js')

block content
  p Inherited Content
```

Rendering the view will generate the following HTML:

```
<!DOCTYPE html>
<html>
<head>
<script src="/one.js"></script>
<script src="/library.js"></script>
<script src="/two.js"></script>
</head>
<body>
<p>Inherited Content</p>
<div id="footer">The original footer</div>
</body>
</html>
```

Notice how the view prepended a new `script` tag `<script src="/one.js"></script>`, and appended a new `script` tag `<script src="/two.js"></script>`, to the original content of the `head` block.

Since we defined a new block for content, the original content block was overwritten by the view's content. And because we did not define a block for the footer block, the original stayed.

Includes and template inheritance are not exclusive to each other. In fact, for complex layouts, you will be able to achieve the most optimal view by using a mixture of both.

Mixins

Mixins are named blocks of code that can be executed to programmatically generate HTML. They work a lot like JavaScript functions, except their syntax is a little different.

Here is a simple mixin that just returns a predefined list:

```
//- Define the mixin
mixin skills_list
  ul
    li Dancing
    li Computer Hacking
    li Nunchucks

//- Call the mixin
mixin skills_list
```

The preceding Jade code will generate the following:

```
<ul>
<li>Dancing</li>
<li>Computer Hacking</li>
<li>Nunchucks</li>
</ul>
```

A less verbose method of calling a mixin is to append the mixin name with a plus (+). So, the preceding mixin can also be called using `+skills_list`.

Mixins can optionally accept arguments and perform logical operations, as shown in the following example.

Assume we have variable named `heroes` in the view, with the following value:

```
[
  {name: 'Fooman', role: 'captain'},
  {name: 'Barman', role: 'entertainer'},
  {name: 'Napman', role: 'hacker'},
  {name: 'Zipman', role: 'collector'}
]
```

Here is the Jade code defining a mixin and calling it from an `each` loop:

```
mixin heroes_list(hero)
  if hero.role == 'captain'
    li Captain #{hero.name}
  else
    li #{hero.name}

ul
  each hero in heroes
    +heroes_list(hero)
```

The preceding code will generate the following HTML:

```
<ul>
<li>Captain Fooman</li>
<li>Barman</li>
<li>Napman</li>
<li>Zipman</li>
</ul>
```

Mixins, like JavaScript functions, can access variables defined outside their block. In the following example, we define an array outside a mixin, but loop through the array in the mixin:

```
skills = ['Dancing', 'Computer Hacking', 'Nunchucks'];

mixin skills_list
  ul
    each skill in skills
      li.skill= skill

+skills_list
```

The preceding code will generate the following:

```
<ul>
<li class="skill">Dancing</li>
```

```
<li class="skill">Computer Hacking</li>
<li class="skill">Nunchucks</li>
</ul>
```

Escaping

We have seen that HTML in variables is escaped by using escaped interpolation constructs `!=` or `!{}`. How about escaping the Jade interpolation constructs `=`, `!=`, `#{}`, and `!{}`?

Jade interpolation constructs can be escaped with the combination of backslash (\) and the `=` HTML entity:

Jade	Rendered HTML
`p` `= message`	`= message`
`p` `  != message`	`!= message`
`p \#{message}`	`#{message}`
`p \!{message}`	`!{message}`
`p \\#{message}`	`\#{message}`
`p \\!{message}`	`\!{message}`

Using the `=` HTML entity code makes Jade render `=` in the browser, rather than interpret it as the Jade interpolation construct.

`#` and `!` are escaped using the popular escape character, backslash (\). If you intend to use \ as a literal, you will need to escape it too with \, as shown in the preceding example.

Comments

Comments in Jade are marked using double slashes (`//`) or double slashes with a trailing hyphen (`//-`). The former comments show up in the HTML as HTML comments, while the latter remain in the view file and are not rendered in the HTML.

Tags nested within a comment will either be commented in the HTML or not be rendered at all, depending on the comment type.

Here are some examples to help you understand how comments work in Jade:

Jade	HTML
// Here is a comment	<!-- Here is a comment-->
p Howdy?	<p>Howdy?</p>
//- This comment will not be shown in the HTML	<p>Something interesting</p>
p Something interesting	
// p This paragraph will be commented out	<!-- <p>This paragraph will be commented out</p> -->
//- p This paragraph won't even show up in the HTML	

Jade even supports Internet Explorer's conditional comments:

```
// if lt 8
  script
    alert('Upgrade your browser!');
```

will render:

```
<!--[if lt 8]>
    <script>alert('Upgrade your browser!');</script>
<![endif]-->
```

Summary

In this chapter, we learned about the Jade templating language. We now know how to create modular views for our app and use the various Jade constructs to customize the structure and contents of the views.

Now that we know Jade in detail, it is time to learn more about its CSS counterpart—Stylus. In the next chapter, we will study Stylus in great detail.

6
The Stylus CSS Preprocessor

Stylus is the recommended CSS preprocessor for Express. It comes with an intuitive syntax for generating CSS and a flexible programming language to manage the dynamics of the CSS generation process.

Using Stylus saves a lot of time during development and maintenance. You will learn the following in this chapter:

- How to enable Stylus in Express
- Understand the Stylus CSS syntax
- How to use the programming capabilities of Stylus

Introduction

Stylus is a CSS preprocessor—a tool for generating CSS in a more efficient and dynamic manner. It comes with a logical syntax for generating CSS style definition blocks, and a programming language to make the CSS generation process very dynamic.

> Although, we cover most aspects of Stylus in this chapter, for a complete coverage of the topic visit the official website at `http://learnboost.github.io/stylus/`.

Stylus files have a `.styl` file extension. The contents of these files are parsed and converted to CSS code when the corresponding `.css` file is requested by a user agent.

Stylus CSS syntax isn't very different from regular CSS. In fact, regular CSS language is valid Stylus too, because Stylus is a superset of CSS. All Stylus does is add some dynamic capabilities to the plain old CSS. However, colons, semicolons, commas, and braces are optional in Stylus.

A very important difference between CSS and Stylus is that whitespace is significant in Stylus. In fact, we use indentation (tabs or spaces) to create CSS selector blocks.

Here are some examples to help you get some idea about how Stylus looks and works:

Stylus	CSS

// This is a comment
strong {
  color: #999;
}
	strong {
	  color: #999;
	}

// Braces and semicolons are optional
strong
  color: #999
	strong {
	  color: #999;
	}

// Colons are optional
strong
  color #999
	strong {
	  color: #999;
	}

strong, b
  color: #999
	strong,
	b {
	  color: #999;
	}

strong,
b
  color: #999
	strong,
	b {
	  color: #999;
	}

// Commas are optional
strong
b
.important
  color: #999
	strong,
	b,
	.important {
	  color: #999;
	}

// Indented hierarchy
#content
  font: 14px Arial
  width: 300px
 	
  .notice
    border: 1px dotted #ccc
    border-radius: 3px
    padding: 3px
 	
  strong
    color: #bababa
	#content {
	  font: 14px Arial;
	  width: 300px;
	}
	#content .notice {
	  border: 1px dotted
	#ccc;
	  border-radius: 3px;
	  padding: 3px;
	}
	#content strong {
	  color: #bababa;
	}

Stylus	CSS

<pre>// A variable
warning-color = #dd0000
 	
.warn
  color: warning-color
 	
#footer .error
  color: warning-color</pre>
	<pre>.warn {
	  color: #d00;
	}
	#footer .error {
	  color: #d00;
	}</pre>

<pre>// Programming constructs
headers = 1 2 3 4 5 6
pi = 22/7
base = 200
 	
for h in headers
  h{h}
    font-size: floor(base / (pi * h))px</pre>
	<pre>h1 {
	  font-size: 63px;
	}
	h2 {
	  font-size: 31px;
	}
	h3 {
	  font-size: 21px;
	}
	h4 {
	  font-size: 15px;
	}
	h5 {
	  font-size: 12px;
	}
	h6 {
	  font-size: 10px;
	}</pre>

<pre>// Conditionals
mode = dev
 	
if mode == dev
  .debug
    display: block
else
  .debug
    display: none</pre>
	<pre>.debug {
	  display: block;
	}</pre>

Following these examples, you will be able to write Stylus code, just enough to add some dynamism and flexibility in your CSS. But there is more to Stylus, let's find out more about its syntax, capabilities, and features.

Enabling Stylus in Express

Although Stylus is the recommended CSS preprocessor for Express, it does not come baked into Express by default. However, adding Stylus support in Express is very easy.

The first step is to install the Stylus `npm` package in the application directory:

```
$ npm install stylus
```

The next step is to include the Stylus middleware and the `static` middleware in the application. It is recommended to add them right after the `router` middleware:

```
app.use(app.router);
app.use(require('stylus').middleware('./public'));
app.use(express.static('./public'));
```

By passing a single parameter to the `middleware()` method, we specify where to find the Stylus files. When a request for a CSS file is made to the app, it will look for the corresponding Stylus file in this directory.

The `static` middleware is required for serving the generated CSS files, along with other static resources from the app.

Stylus accepts more options than just a location for the stylus files. These options can be specified by passing an object, instead of the directory path to the `middleware()` method.

```
app.use(require('stylus').middleware({
  src: './public,
  compress: true
}));
```

The following table shows all the possible options:

Name	Description
`serve`	Serves Stylus files from the `dest` directory.
`force`	Forces recompilation of the Stylus files for every request.
`src`	The path from which to find the Stylus files. This directory also is the root path of the CSS files requested by the browser.
`dest`	The path to which to output the compiled CSS files. If not specified, defaults to `src`.
`compile`	A custom compile function.
`compress`	Minifies the generated CSS.

Name	Description
`firebug`	Generates debug info for the FireStylus Firebug plugin.
`linenos`	Shows commented Stylus line number.

Using Stylus does not mean that we include the Stylus files in our HTML. We include the CSS files as usual, and Stylus takes care of generating the CSS code from the corresponding Stylus file. Everything happens seamlessly in the background.

We create the Stylus file and continue to include the CSS file as usual.

In regular HTML:

```
<link rel="stylesheet" href="/stylesheets/style.css">
```

In Jade:

```
link(rel='stylesheet', href='/stylesheets/style.css')
```

Using the Stylus filter, Stylus code can be defined right in a Jade file too:

Jade / Stylus	HTML / CSS

`head`
`  :stylus`
`    warning-color = #dd0000`
`    .warn`
`      color: warning-color`
`    #footer .error`
`      color: warning-color`
	`<head>`
	`<style type="text/css">`
	`    .warn {`
	`      color: #d00;`
	`    }`
	`    #footer .error {`
	`      color: #d00;`
	`    }`
	`</style>`
	`</head>`

When using the Stylus filter in Jade, you don't have to use the `style` tag to create the `style` tag to include the Stylus code. The Stylus filter will create the `style` tag with the right attribute for you.

Selectors

Stylus does not change the original syntax of CSS selectors—IDs are selected using `#`, classes using `.`, direct children using `>`, and so on. It just adds some additional features on top of CSS to make defining style declarations easier and dynamic.

Selector blocks

Selectors and style declarations in Stylus are superset of the standard CSS selectors and style declarations; hence regular CSS is valid Stylus:

```
#content {
  color: #999;
  padding: 5px;
  box-shadow: 5px 5px 1px #ccc;
}
```

However, colons, semicolons, commas, and braces are optional in Stylus:

```
#content
  color #999
  padding 5px
  box-shadow 5px 5px 1px #ccc
```

Omitting colons can make things a little confusing, so you might want to keep the colons to help in visually demarcate properties and values:

```
#content
  color: #999
  padding: 5px
  box-shadow: 5px 5px 1px #ccc
```

Omitting the braces comes with a price—we now use indentations to define the selector blocks. You can use either tabs or spaces for indentation. Choose whichever you find comfortable and stick to it.

Stylus doesn't validate the name of selectors, properties, and values; it is just a language for making CSS dynamic. It will render anything as long as it doesn't interfere with its syntax, as shown in the following example. So, watch out!

Stylus	CSS

`foo -bar`
`  lul: wut`
	`foo -bar {`
	`  lul: wut;`
	`}`

Hierarchy

Stylus has a very logical implementation of defining hierarchical CSS definition blocks. You create the root block and nest other selectors within it with the appropriate indentation.

Take a look at this example:

Stylus	CSS

`#container`
`  width: 600px`
`  div`
`    padding: 3px`
`  .block`
`    width: 50%`
`    strong`
`      color: #ccc`
	`#container {`
	`  width: 600px;`
	`}`
	`#container div {`
	`  padding: 3px;`
	`}`
	`#container .block {`
	`  width: 50%;`
	`}`
	`#container .block strong {`
	`  color: #ccc;`
	`}`

Using the `&` character, you can refer to the parent selector from a block. Using this technique can greatly reduce the verbosity and make style declarations a lot more logical, as shown here:

Stylus	CSS

`.block`
`  padding: 5px`
`  color: #ccc`
`  strong`
`    color: #555`
`&.special`
`    border: 1px solid #900`
`    padding: 3px`
`&:hover`
`    border-color: #d00`
	`.block {`
	`  padding: 5px;`
	`  color: #ccc;`
	`}`
	`.block strong {`
	`  color: #555;`
	`}`
	`.block.special {`
	`  border: 1px solid #900;`
	`  padding: 3px;`
	`}`
	`.block:hover {`
	`  border-color: #d00;`
	`}`

Rules

Stylus implements a superset of various CSS rules, and includes some of its own.

@import

`@import` can either be used to import CSS or Stylus files. When importing CSS files, the rule works in the regular CSS context. When importing Stylus files, the contents of the included files are parsed and included in the generated CSS file.

The import path is relative to the directory of the file applying the import rule.

Importing a CSS file is done just by using the regular CSS `@import` rule:

```
@import "common.css"
```

If the file extension is `.styl` or it is omitted, it is assumed to be a Style file, and the content of the included file is rendered in the generated file.

Say, this is the content of `special.styl`:

```
.special
  border: 1px solid red
```

And this, the content of `style.styl`:

```
@import "special"
```

When `style.css` is called, the following will be generated:

```
.special {
  border: 1px solid #f00;
}
```

To modularize Stylus imports, we can use indexed directories. In such cases, we just have to mention the name of the directory to include.

Let's say we have a directory named `mobile` in the `src` directory, with two files `index.styl` and `ui.styl` in it.

Content of `index.styl`:

```
.mobile
  width: 100%

@import "ui"
```

Content of `ui.styl`:

```
button
  padding: 2 5px
  font: 12px Tahoma
```

The result of rendering `style.styl` is shown in the following table:

style.styl	style.css

`@import "mobile"`	`.mobile {`
	`  width: 100%;`
	`}`
	`button {`
	`  padding: 2 5px;`
	`  font: 12px Tahoma;`
	`}`

Another advantage of using indexed directories is that the files in the directories can be individually included from other files, as shown here:

```
@import "mobile/ui"
@import "mobile/layout"
```

@media

The `@media` rule works like the regular CSS rule, except it is less verbose:

Stylus	CSS

`@media print`
`  #header`
`  #footer`
`    display none`
	`@media print {`
	`  #header,`
	`  #footer {`
	`    display: none;`
	`  }`
	`}`

`@media (min-width: 700px)`
`  #info-panel`
`    display: block`
	`@media (min-width: 700px) {`
	`  #info-panel {`
	`    display: block;`
	`  }`
	`}`

Stylus	CSS

`@media all and (min-width:800px) and (max-width:1023px)`
`  #extra-blogroll, #feedburner-link`
`    display: none`
	`@media all and (min-width:800px) and (max-width:1023px) {`
	`  #extra-blogroll,`
	`  #feedburner-link {`
	`    display: none;`
	`  }`
	`}`

@font-face

The `@font-face` rule is a friendly wrapper on top of CSS' `@font-face`:

Stylus	CSS

`@font-face`
` font-family Neo`
` font-style normal`
` src local("Neo Sans"), url(fonts/Neo-Sans.ttf)`
 	
`.font-neo`
` font-family Neo`
	`@font-face {`
	`  font-family: Neo;`
	`  font-style: normal;`
	`  src: local("Neo Sans"), url("fonts/Neo-Sans.ttf");`
	`}`
	`.font-neo {`
	`  font-family: Neo;`
	`}`

@keyframes

The `@keyframe` rule is useful for generating vendor-specific keyframe rules for CSS. There is a variable named `vendors` in Stylus, which is a list of vendors that defaults to `moz webkit o ms official`.

Stylus	CSS

`@keyframes foo`
`  from`
`    width: 50px`
`  to`
`    width: 100px`
	`@-moz-keyframes foo {`
	`  0% {`
	`    width: 50px;`
	`  }`
	
	`  100% {`
	`    width: 100px;`
	`  }`
	`}`
	`@-webkit-keyframes foo {`
	`  0% {`
	`    width: 50px;`
	`  }`
	
	`  100% {`
	`    width: 100px;`
	`  }`
	`}`
	`@-o-keyframes foo {`
	`  0% {`
	`    width: 50px;`
	`  }`
	
	`  100% {`
	`    width: 100px;`
	`  }`
	`}`
	`@-ms-keyframes foo {`
	`  0% {`
	`    width: 50px;`
	`  }`
	
	`  100% {`
	`    width: 100px;`
	`  }`
	`}`
	`@keyframes foo {`
	`  0% {`
	`    width: 50px;`
	`  }`
	
	`  100% {`
	`    width: 100px;`
	`  }`
	`}`

By overwriting the `vendors` variable, you can customize the vendor prefixes in the generated CSS:

Stylus	CSS

<pre>vendors = official webkit
 	
@keyframes bar
  from
    width: 50px
  to
    width: 100px</pre>
	<pre>@keyframes bar {
	  0% {
	    width: 50px;
	  }
	
	  100% {
	    width: 100px;
	  }
	}
	@-webkit-keyframes bar {
	  0% {
	    width: 50px;
	  }
	
	  100% {
	    width: 100px;
	  }
	}</pre>

@extend

`@extend` is a Stylus-specific rule that makes re-using CSS style definitions very intuitive. Using this rule, you can include predefined styles in a style block.

Make sure that the style you are trying to extend is already defined or else you will encounter an error.

Stylus	CSS

<pre>.content
  padding: 10px
  font-size: 14px
 	
#message
  @extends .content
  margin: 5px 0</pre>
	<pre>.content,
	#message {
	  padding: 10px;
	  font-size: 14px;
	}
	#message {
	  margin: 5px 0;
	}</pre>

<table>
<tr><th>Stylus</th><th>CSS</th></tr>
<tr><td><pre>
.message
  padding: 10px
  font: 14px Helvetica
  border: 1px solid #eee

.warning
  @extends .message
  border-color: yellow
  background: yellow

.error
  @extends .message
  border-color: red
  background: red
</pre></td><td><pre>
.message,
.warning,
.error {
  padding: 10px;
  font: 14px Helvetica;
  border: 1px solid #eee;
}
.warning {
  border-color: #ff0;
  background: #ff0;
}
.error {
  border-color: #f00;
  background: #f00;
}
</pre></td></tr>
</table>

@css

Anything defined within a `@css` rule is understood as literal CSS. None of the Stylus-specific constructs work within this rule. You can use this rule in those rare situations when you need to use plain old CSS within Stylus.

Here are some examples to help you understand how `@css` works:

<table>
<tr><th>Stylus</th><th>CSS</th></tr>
<tr><td><pre>
@css {
  #container {
    color: #333;
    padding: 3px;
  }
}
</pre></td><td><pre>
#container {
  color: #333;
  padding: 3px;
}
</pre></td></tr>
</table>

<table>
<tr><th>Stylus</th><th>CSS</th></tr>
<tr><td><pre>
light_gray = #ccc
dark_gray = #555
bright_red = #f00

.block
  padding: 5px
  color: light_gray
  strong
    color: dark_gray
&:hover
    border-color: bright_red
</pre></td><td><pre>
.block {
  padding: 5px;
  color: #ccc;
}
.block strong {
  color: #555;
}
.block:hover {
  border-color:
#f00;
}
</pre></td></tr>
<tr><td><pre>
@css {
  light_gray = #ccc
  dark_gray = #555
  bright_red = #f00

  .block
    padding: 5px
    color: light_gray
    strong
      color: dark_gray
&:hover
      border-color: bright_red
}
</pre></td><td><pre>
light_gray = #ccc
dark_gray = #555
bright_red = #f00

.block
  padding: 5px
  color: light_gray
  strong
    color: dark_
gray
&:hover
    border-color:
bright_red
</pre></td></tr>
</table>

Programmability

Stylus provides a relatively minimal but efficient programming language in addition to the CSS syntax. Using this programming language, you can make CSS generation dynamic and more flexible.

The Stylus programming language is limited in many ways, and some implementation may still be buggy due its young age.

Variables

Although the data type is not strongly defined in Stylus, variables can be broadly classified as literals, lists, and tuples.

Stylus variable identifiers can start with any alphabetical character: `$`, `-`, or `_` and contain alphanumeric characters along with the aforementioned characters.

The following are some examples of variables in Stylus:

```
$font-weight = bold
num = 100
vendors = moz webkit ms
-height = (num/5)px
_width = 200
```

Literals

The most common data type in Stylus is literals. Literals are strings of text that are not lists or tuples, and are interpreted literally.

The following table demonstrates how literal variables can be used in CSS declarations:

<table>
<tr><th>Stylus</th><th>CSS</th></tr>
<tr><td><pre>fixed-width = 800px
$font-weight = bold
num = 100
-height = (num/5)px
_width = 200
font-family = "Comic Sans MS"

#content
  width: fixed-width
  font-weight: $font-weight
  height: -height
  font-size: (num)px
  font-family: font-family
  .message
    width: (_width)px</pre></td><td><pre>#content {
  width: 800px;
  font-weight: bold;
  height: 20px;
  font-size: 100px;
  font-family: "Comic Sans
MS";
}
#content .message {
  width: 200px;
}</pre></td></tr>
</table>

Stylus variables, as expected, can be used seamlessly within other variables too:

Stylus	CSS

`font-size = 14px`
`base-font = font-size Arial`
 	
`#content`
`  font: base-font, sans-serif`
	`#content {`
	`  font: 14px Arial, sans-serif;`
	`}`

If you try to use a variable that is not defined, the literal name of the variable will be used instead of `undefined` or `null`:

Stylus	CSS

`#content`
`  width: $width`
 	
`$width = 100px`
`#message`
`  width: $width`
	`#content {`
	`  width: $width;`
	`}`
	`#message {`
	`  width: 100px;`
	`}`

When you assign a value to a CSS property, the property is available as a variable, which can be referred to by prefixing the property name with `@`:

Stylus	CSS

`#content`
`  width:800px`
`  height (@width/2)px`
`  margin: 2px 5px`
`  padding: @margin`
	`#content {`
	`  width: 800px;`
	`  height: 400px;`
	`  margin: 2px 5px;`
	`  padding: 2px 5px;`
	`}`

The `@` variables are looked up from inner to outer block, and when not defined, they return null.

While using variables in style values is pretty straightforward, trying to use them in property names can be confusing at first:

<table>
<tr><th>Stylus</th><th>CSS</th></tr>
<tr><td><pre>prefix = chan

#(prefix)-one
  width: 10%</pre></td><td><pre>#(prefix)-one {
  width: 10%;
}</pre></td></tr>
</table>

Use {} instead of `()` to interpolate variables in CSS properties. The following examples show how to do that:

<table>
<tr><th>Stylus</th><th>CSS</th></tr>
<tr><td><pre>prefix = chan

#{prefix}-one
  width: 20%

#{prefix}-two
  width: 80%</pre></td><td><pre>#chan-one {
  width: 20%;
}
#chan-two {
  width: 80%;
}</pre></td></tr>
<tr><td><pre>chans = one two three

for chan in chans
  #chan-{chan}
    width: (floor(100/
length(chans)))px</pre></td><td><pre>#chan-one {
  width: 33px;
}
#chan-two {
  width: 33px;
}
#chan-three {
  width: 33px;
}</pre></td></tr>
</table>

Special characters can be escaped using backslash (\), and operations are forced upon on otherwise literals by using (), where applicable, as shown in the following examples:

<table>
<tr><th>Stylus</th><th>CSS</th></tr>
<tr><td><pre>.dynamic
  width: calc(100% \/ 2)

.blocks
  height: (20px/2)
  width: 60px/3</pre></td><td><pre>.dynamic {
  width: calc(100%/2);
}
.blocks {
  height: 10px;
  width: 60px/3;
}</pre></td></tr>
</table>

Lists

Lists are similar to arrays in JavaScript, except that they are represented by nothing but a string of space-delimited characters. Stylus provides various built-in functions and a construct to loop through lists.

To create a list, you just assign a list of space-delimited characters to a variable:

```
fonts = Times Arial Helvetica
```

If you need to include items with spaces in them, just quote them:

```
fonts = Times Arial Helvetica "Comic Sans MS"
```

Items in a list start with an index of `0`, and can be accessed by their index number:

<table>
<tr><th>Stylus</th><th>CSS</th></tr>
<tr><td><pre>fonts = Arial Times Helvetica

.funny
  font-family: fonts[1]</pre></td><td><pre>.funny {
  font-family: Times;
}</pre></td></tr>
</table>

Lists can be iterated by value alone or along with the index number:

<table>
<tr><th>Stylus</th><th>CSS</th></tr>
<tr><td><pre>hidden = header footer

for tag in hidden
  {tag}
    display: none

fonts = Times Arial Helvetica
for font, i in fonts
  h{i+1}
    font-family: font</pre></td><td><pre>header {
  display: none;
}
footer {
  display: none;
}
h1 {
  font-family: Times;
}
h2 {
  font-family: Arial;
}
h3 {
  font-family: Helvetica;
}</pre></td></tr>
</table>

Stylus comes with a set of built-in functionalities for manipulating arrays:

Function	Description
`push(list, a, b, ...)`	Adds new items to the list at the end
`append(list, a, b, ...)`	Alias of `push()`
`unshift(list, a, b, ...)`	Adds new items to the list at the front
`join(deliminator, values)`	Joins the values with the deliminator

Tuples

Tuples are another kind of list, but they are meant for storing related data. Although a single tuple can be used in a program, they are often used as a list of tuples.

Unlike Python tuples, Stylus tuples are mutable; meaning you can change their contents.

To create a tuple, just assign a list of space-delimited strings within parentheses to a variable:

```
font = (Helvetica 10px)
```

If you need to include items with spaces in them, just quote them:

```
font = ("Comic Sans MS" 12px)
```

Tuples are a lot like lists, except in their purpose. All the built-in list functions can be applied to tuples too. However, tuples are not meant to be used like lists. Tuples are commonly used for containing related data within a list:

Stylus	CSS

`fonts = (Arial 10px) (Tahoma 12px) (Helvetica 14px)`
`#content`
`  font-family: fonts[2][0]`
`  font-size: fonts[2][1]`
	`#content {`
	`  font-family: Helvetica;`
	`  font-size: 14px;`
	`}`

Listed tuples

Although, technically not a separate data type, listed tuples deserve a separate section because of the way they work. Listed tuples are lists of tuples with two significant values, which are understood as key-value pairs.

Stylus does not recognize tuples with a single item in it as an iterable, if you try to loop through a tuple with a single item, it will throw an error.

Listed tuples support these two built-in functions:

Function	Description
`keys(list)`	Returns the keys of the listed tuples. Essentially returns index `0` of the listed tuples.
`values(list)`	Returns the value of the listed tuples. Essentially returns index `1` of the listed tuples.

Mixins

Mixins are dynamic blocks of CSS style declarations, which can be added to a style definition block. They are invoked at the style declaration level as a statement:

Stylus

```
common-border-radius()
  -webkit-border-radius: 5px
  -moz-border-radius: 5px
  border-radius: 5px

#content
  width: 100px
  common-border-radius()
```

CSS

```
#content {
  width: 100px;
  -webkit-border-radius: 5px;
  -moz-border-radius: 5px;
  border-radius: 5px;
}
```

Mixins can accept arguments, and the arguments can have default values:

Stylus

```
set-font(size, line-height,
family=Times)
  font: size/line-height family

#content
  set-font(14px, 15px)

#message
  set-font(12px, 12px, Arial)
```

CSS

```
#content {
  font: 14px/15px Times;
}
#message {
  font: 12px/12px Arial;
}
```

If you define your mixins to accept arguments, either set their default values, or pass the arguments when invoking them, or else Stylus will throw an error.

Mixins can be used in a transparent manner, as if they were CSS property names. Basically, you can omit the braces and commas:

Stylus	CSS

`set-font(size, line-height, family=Times)`
`  font: size/line-height family`
 	
`#content`
`  set-font: 14px 15px`
 	
`#message`
`  set-font: 12px 12px Arial`
	`#content {`
	`  font: 14px/15px Times;`
	`}`
	`#message {`
	`  font: 12px/12px Arial;`
	`}`

You can use the `arguments` local variable in a mixin to refer to the whole body of the arguments passed to a mixin.

Stylus	CSS

`set-font()`
`  font: arguments`
 	
`#message`
`  set-font: 12px/12px Arial, sans-serif;`
	`#message {`
	`  font: 12px/12px Arial, sans-serif;`
	`}`

Mixins can be named after a CSS property name, and when referred within itself, it does recurse:

Stylus	CSS

`width(p)`
`  width: (100% - p)`
 	
`#message`
`  width: 10%`
	`#message {`
	`  width: 90%;`
	`}`

`x-width(p)`
`  x-width: (100% - p)`
 	
`#message`
`  x-width: 10%`
	`#message {`
	`  x-width: 90%;`
	`}`

Functions

Functions are defined like mixins, but they return a value instead of a set of CSS property definitions. While mixins are invoked as a statement, functions are used in expressions:

Stylus	CSS

`get-color(p)`
`  if p > 5`
`    return #f00`
`  else`
`    return #0f0`
 	
`get-font()`
`  return Arial`
 	
`.note`
`  color: get-color(5)`
`  font: 12px get-font()`
 	
`// return keyword is optional`
`width-a()`
`  100px`
 	
`#content`
`  width: width-a()`
	`.note {`
	`  color: #0f0;`
	`  font: 12px Arial;`
	`}`
	
	`#content {`
	`  width: 100px;`
	`}`

By using conflicting function names with the built-in functions, you can overwrite them, so be careful.

Comments

Stylus supports JavaScript-style single line comments on individual lines or after the property definitions. These comments are not included in the generated CSS:

Stylus	CSS

`// Styles for .description`
`.description`
`&.error`
`    color: #ff0000 // brightest red`
`  .error`
`    color: #dd0000 // darker red`
	`.description.error {`
	`  color: #f00;`
	`}`
	`.description .error {`
	`  color: #d00;`
	`}`

Note that Stylus, currently, does not support inline comments on selectors. The following Stylus code will generate broken CSS:

Stylus	CSS

`.description // Styles for`
`.description`
`&.error`
`    color: #ff0000 // brightest`
`red`
`  .error`
`    color: #dd0000 // darker red`
	`.description // Styles for`
	`.description.error {`
	`  color: #f00;`
	`}`
	`.description // Styles for`
	`.description .error {`
	`  color: #d00;`
	`}`

Stylus also supports the conventional CSS comments. These comments, however, are included in the generated CSS:

Stylus	CSS

`/*`
`* This is`
`* a multiline`
`* comment`
`*/`
`h1`
`  font-size: 30px`
	`/*`
	`* This is`
	`* a multiline`
	`* comment`
	`*/`
	`h1 {`
	`  font-size: 30px;`
	`}`

To suppress multiline comments in CSS, set the Stylus `compress` option to `true`:

```
app.use(require('stylus').middleware({
  src: __dirname + '/public',
  compress: true
}));
```

When the `compress` option is set to `true`, multiline comments will not be generated and the CSS will be minified. In case you want to keep a multiline comment, append `!` to the opening comment marker:

Stylus	CSS

`/*!`
`* Copyright © 2013`
`* Hack Sparrow`
`*/`
`h1`
`  font-size: 30px`
	`/*`
	`* Copyright © 2013`
	`* Hack Sparrow`
	`*/`
	`h1 {`
	`  font-size: 30px;`
	`}`

Operators

The following is a list of operators supported by the Stylus programming language:

Operator	Description
`[]`	Subscript
`!`	Logical NOT
`+`	Unary plus
`-`	Unary minus
`is defined`	Checks if variable is defined
`**`	Exponent
`*`	Multiplication
`/`	Division
`%`	Modulus
`+`	Addition
`-`	Subtraction
`n1..n2`	Inclusive range. Generates a list of numbers from `n1` to `n2`, including `n2`.
`n1...n2`	Exclusive range. Generates a list of numbers from `n1` to `n2`, excluding `n2`.
`<=`	Less than or equal to
`>=`	More than or equal to

<table>
<tr><th>Operator</th><th>Description</th></tr>
<tr><td><code><</code></td><td>Less than</td></tr>
<tr><td><code>></code></td><td>More than</td></tr>
<tr><td><code>in</code></td><td>Checks if value is in a list or tuple</td></tr>
<tr><td><code>==</code></td><td>Equal to</td></tr>
<tr><td><code>is</code></td><td>Designer-friendly syntax for <code>==</code></td></tr>
<tr><td><code>!=</code></td><td>Not equal to</td></tr>
<tr><td><code>is not</code></td><td>Designer-friendly syntax for <code>!=</code></td></tr>
<tr><td><code>isnt</code></td><td>Alias of is not</td></tr>
<tr><td><code>&&</code></td><td>Logical AND</td></tr>
<tr><td><code>and</code></td><td>Designer-friendly alias for <code>&&</code></td></tr>
<tr><td><code>||</code></td><td>Logical OR</td></tr>
<tr><td><code>or</code></td><td>Designer-friendly alias for <code>||</code></td></tr>
<tr><td><code>=</code></td><td>Assignment</td></tr>
<tr><td><code>?:</code></td><td>Ternary operator</td></tr>
<tr><td><code>:=</code></td><td>Conditional assignment</td></tr>
<tr><td><code>?=</code></td><td>Alias of <code>:=</code></td></tr>
<tr><td><code>+=</code></td><td>Addition assignment</td></tr>
<tr><td><code>-=</code></td><td>Subtraction assignment</td></tr>
<tr><td><code>*=</code></td><td>Multiplication assignment</td></tr>
<tr><td><code>/=</code></td><td>Division assignment</td></tr>
<tr><td><code>%=</code></td><td>Modulo assignment</td></tr>
<tr><td><code>not</code></td><td>Designer-friendly syntax for <code>!</code></td></tr>
</table>

Currently, there are no increment (++) and decrement (--) operators in Stylus.

Conditionals

Stylus provides two conditional checks for performing logical operations.

if, else if, and else

The `if`, `else if`, and `else` construct works like in JavaScript, except you omit the braces and use indentions to create the conditional block:

Stylus	CSS

<pre>env = development
 	
body
  if env == development
    font-family: Arial
  else if env == production
    font-family: Helvetica
  else
    font-family: Times</pre>
	<pre>body {
	  font-family: Arial;
	}</pre>

unless

The `unless` conditional is an alternative way for checking for Boolean false:

Stylus	CSS

<pre>env = development
 	
unless env == production
  body
    font-family: Arial
env = production
 	
unless env == production
  body
    font-family: Arial</pre>
	<pre>body {
	  font-family: Arial;
	}</pre>

Built-in functions

Stylus comes with a large number of built-in functions to perform common operations on objects, especially related to CSS.

The following is a list of some useful in-built functions:

Function	Description
`red(color)`	Returns the red component of the color
`green(color)`	Returns the green component of the color
`blue(color)`	Returns the blue component of the color
`alpha(color)`	Returns the alpha component of the color
`dark(color)`	Checks if the color is dark
`light(color)`	Checks if the color is light
`hue(color)`	Returns the hue of the color
`saturation(color)`	Returns the saturation of the color
`lightness(color)`	Returns the lightness of the color
`invert(color)`	Inverts the color
`saturate(color, amount)`	Saturates the color by the given amount
`desaturate(color, amount)`	Desaturates the color by the given amount
`lighten(color, amount)`	Lightens the color by the given amount
`darken(color, amount)`	Darkens the color by the given amount
`match(pattern, string)`	Checks if the string matches the regular expression pattern
`abs(value)`	Returns the absolute value
`ceil(value)`	Rounds the value to the nearest upper value integer
`floor(value)`	Rounds the value to the nearest lower value integer
`round(value)`	Rounds the value to the nearest integer
`even(value)`	Checks if the numeric component is even
`odd(value)`	Checks if the numeric component is odd
`unquote(string)`	Removes quotes from the string
`p(expression)`	Prints the value of the expression to `stdout`

Summary

Now we know how to generate CSS using the Stylus preprocessor. We learned about the Stylus syntax and programming to make CSS generation more efficient and dynamic.

So far what we learned has been mostly static interactions with the server. In the next chapter, we will learn how to make things more dynamic with the use of forms, cookies, and sessions.

7
Forms, Cookies, and Sessions

Any website that is beyond simple static web pages is likely to have forms, support file uploads, and maintain some form of data state. Forms, cookies, and sessions are all interrelated and work together to accomplish the common goal of creating a dynamic experience in a web app.

This chapter is about enabling these features in an Express app. Here is what you will learn in this chapter:

- How to submit forms using various methods
- How to create, read, update, and delete cookies
- How to create sessions
- How to create, read, update, and delete session variables

Using forms to submit data

The HTML form provides two methods for submitting data to the backend using the GET and the POST methods. In this section, we will find out how to read data submitted via these methods.

> Although GET and POST are the conventional methods of form submission in HTML, using the **methodOverride** middleware in Express, we can submit forms using any valid HTTP method.

GET forms are submitted using the GET HTTP method and the form data is sent in the query string of the URL specified in the `action` attribute of the form.

POST forms are submitted using the POST HTTP method and the form data is sent in the body of the HTTP request.

POST forms come in two varieties: `application/x-www-form-urlencoded` and `multipart/form-data`. The former uses `urlencoded` string for sending data to the server; it is a lot like the GET query string, except the data is sent in the HTTP body. The latter uses a deliminator to send large chunks of data in the HTTP body, and is the version that is used for uploading files.

For those curious ones, here is a quick summary of the important differences between GET and POST methods of form submission:

GET	POST
Form data is sent in the query string. Hence, it is visible in the browser's address bar.	Form data is sent in the HTTP body. Therefore, it is not visible in the address bar.
There is a limit to how much data that can be sent via the GET method.	The amount of data that can be sent using the POST method is virtually limitless.
Cannot be used for uploading files.	Can be used for uploading files.
Cannot use the same URL for handling the form, without having to add additional logic.	Can use the same URL for handling the form by defining a separate route using the `post()` method.

Now that we know about the various ways by which HTML forms can be submitted, let's find out how to handle the various types of form submissions.

Handling GET submissions

Let's create a route and view for a search form. We will set this form to be submitted via the GET method by specifying it in its `method` attribute:

```
!!! 5
html
  head
    title #{title}
    link(rel='stylesheet', href='/stylesheets/style.css')
  body
    h1 #{title}
    p Enter the name to search for.

    form(action='/search-result', method='get')
      label Name
```

```
        input(type='text', name='name')
        input(type='hidden', name='source', value='web')
        input(type='submit', value='Search')
```

Create an appropriate CSS file for the view. The rendered HTML of the Jade view is shown in the following screenshot:

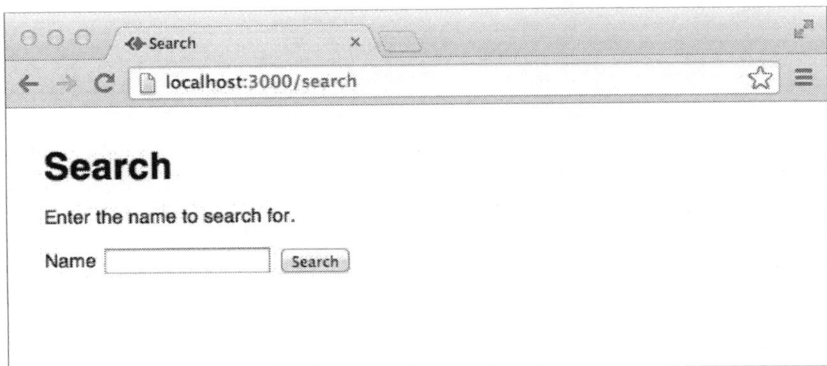

When the form is submitted, the browser will be redirected to its action URL with the query string, which might look like `http://localhost:3000/search-result?name=Captain&source=web`.

Reading form data

All form data submitted via the GET method is available in the `query` property of the request object (`req.query`), at their corresponding keys. For example, if the form had a parameter named `color`, its value will be available at `req.query.color`, and so on.

Trying to read a non-existent key will return undefined, because we are dealing with regular JavaScript objects, and that's the expected behavior.

Let's create a route to handle our form submission. We won't render a view or do anything fancy, let's just read the values and print them:

```
app.get('/search-result', function(req, res) {
  var name = req.query.name;
  var source = req.query.source;
  console.log('Searching for: ' + name);
  console.log('From: ' + source);
  res.send(name + ' : ' + source);
});
```

In case, a GET parameter contains characters that cannot be used as a JavaScript identifier name, you can use a subscript notation to read the value:

```
var firstname = req.query['first name'];
```

Reading data submitted via a GET form is as easy as looking for them in the `req.query` object.

Reading URL query parameters

When it comes to data, GET form submissions are nothing more than URLs with query strings constructed out of the form parameters. Which means, we actually don't need a form to make such requests; they can be crafted in the address bar manually.

Processing a manually-crafted query string is no different from processing one generated by a form. No matter how the query string was created, the parameters will be available in the `req.query` object.

Here is an example of a manually-crafted query string:

```
http://localhost:3000/search-result?q=JavaScript&l=CA&e=10
```

And here is the route and the handler, which reads the data from the previous query string:

```
app.get('/search-result', function(req, res) {
  var q = req.query.q;
  var l = req.query.l;
  var e = req.query.e;
  console.log('Query:' + q);
  console.log('Location:' + l);
  console.log('Experience:' + e);
  res.json(req.query);
});
```

Handling multiple options

Those new to forms and Express are likely to be stumped at handling multiple selected options—the kind of data you create using multiple checkboxes. The following is a quick example to help you understand how to send multiple options and read them at the backend.

Let's create a view with multiple checkboxes. Notice how all of them share a common value for the `name` attribute. The form will be submitted to `http://localhost:3000/skills-search-result`.

```
!!! 5
html
  head
    title #{title}
    link(rel='stylesheet', href='/stylesheets/style.css')
  body
    h1 #{title}
    p Select the skills to search for.

    form(action='/skills-search-result', method='get')
      h3 Skills
      ul
        li
          input(type='checkbox', name='skills', value='Nunchucks')
          label Nunchucks
        li
          input(type='checkbox', name='skills', value='Hacking')
          label Hacking
        li
          input(type='checkbox', name='skills', value='Dancing')
          label Dancing
        li
          input(type='checkbox', name='skills', value='Shooting')
          label Shooting


      input(type='submit', value='Search')
```

And here is the rendered HTML:

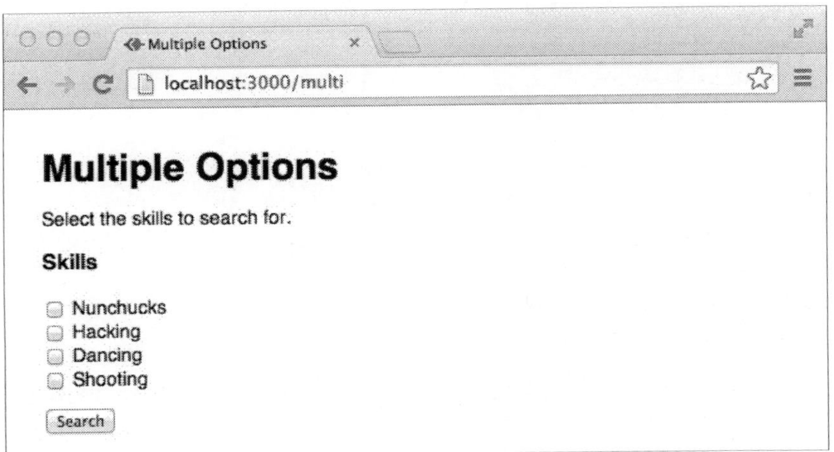

Now, let's create the route for handling the form submission. The `skills` parameter will be available as expected at `req.query.skills`:

```
app.get('/skills-search-result', function(req, res) {
  var skills = req.query.skills;
  console.log('Skills: ');
  skills.forEach(function(skill, i) {
    console.log((i+1) +'. '+ skill);
  });
  res.json(req.query.skills);
});
```

Submitting multiple options is all about setting a common value for the `name` attribute for the set of checkboxes.

Handling POST submissions

The POST method of form submission is the more popular method between GET and POST methods. Consequently, as a backend developer you will be handling more POST forms than GET forms.

Handing POST submissions is different than handling GET submissions and is slightly more advanced. Let's learn how to handle POST form submissions.

Enabling POST data parsing

Unlike GET submissions, which can be processed right out of the box, we need to enable a built-in middleware named `bodyParser` before we can process POST submissions.

Load the `bodyParser` middleware before the `router` middleware to enable POST data handling:

```
app.use(express.bodyParser());
```

Although, the `bodyParser` middleware can be initialized without any parameters, it accepts an optional object with two options that can be used to configure file uploads:

Property	Description
`keepExtensions`	Whether to include the file extension in temporary files. Defaults to `false`, so as not to overwrite a file with the same name.
`uploadDir`	The location where temporary files should be uploaded.

Here is an example of enabling both the options:

```
app.use(express.bodyParser({
  keepExtensions: true,
  uploadDir: './uploads'
}));
```

With the `bodyParser` middleware enabled, we are ready to parse the data submitted by POST forms.

Reading form data

The `bodyParser` middleware will add two new properties: `body` and `files` on the request object and populate them with the key-value pairs of the parameters submitted via the POST request.

Text data from the form is populated in the `req.body` object and files from the form are populated in the `req.files` object.

That is the very basics of handling POST data.

Now it's time to go through some examples and practically experience handling POST forms.

Handling text-only forms

When you don't specify the `encytype` attribute of a form, it is sent to the server with the default `Content-Type` of `application/x-www-form-urlencoded`.

Create a route and the view for a sign-up form:

```
!!! 5
html
  head
    title #{title}
    link(rel='stylesheet', href='/stylesheets/style.css')
  body
    h1 #{title}
    p Enter your name and email address to become a member.

    form(action='/signup', method='post')
      div
        label Name
        input(type='text', name='name')
      div
        label Email
```

```
        input(type='text', name='email')
      div
        input(type='submit')
```

Notice that we have omitted the `enctype` attribute in the form. Here is the rendered view:

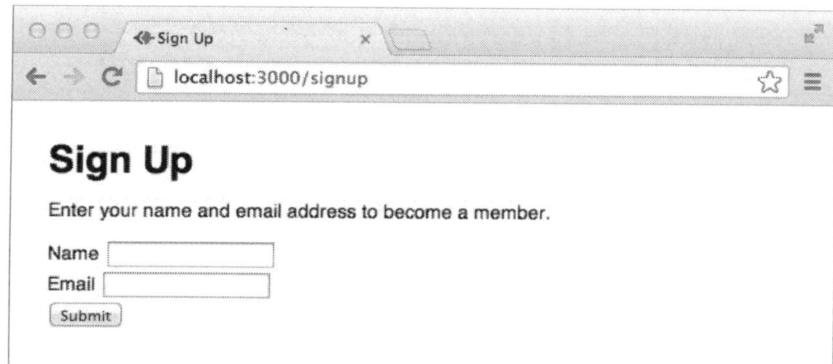

This form will be submitted to `http://localhost:3000/signup`, the same URL that rendered the form. However, it will be submitted via a POST request—making it an altogether different and a valid route.

Let's create the request-handling route for the form. The text data submitted via the form will be available in the `req.body` object:

```
app.post('/signup', function(req, res) {
  var name = req.body.name;
  var email = req.body.email;
  console.log('Name: ' + name);
  console.log('Email: ' + email);
  res.json(req.body);
});
```

In this example, we just print the individual form values to the console and render the `req.body` object in the browser. In a real-world application, you might store these values in a database.

Handling file uploads

To upload files using HTML forms, we need to set the `enctype` attribute of the form to `multipart/form-data`, and of course, include an input element of the type `file`.

Let's update the previous sign-up view to set the `enctype` attribute and include a file input:

```
!!! 5
html
  head
    title #{title}
    link(rel='stylesheet', href='/stylesheets/style.css')
  body
    h1 #{title}
    p Enter your name and email address to become a member.

    form(action='/signup', method='post', enctype='multipart/form-
data')
      div
        label Name
        input(type='text', name='name')
      div
        label Email
        input(type='text', name='email')
      div
        label Profile Image
        input(type='file', name='profile_image')
      div
        input(type='submit')
```

Here is the updated view:

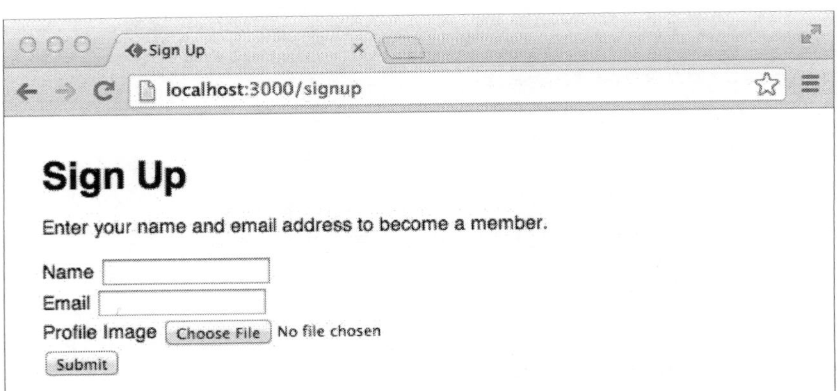

When the form is submitted, the uploaded image will be found in the `req.files` object.

Update the form-handling route for the path:

```
app.post('/signup', function(req, res) {
  var name = req.body.name;
  var email = req.body.email;
  console.log(req.files);
  res.json(req.files);
});
```

Save the relevant files, restart the app, and submit the form.

In the console and the browser, you will see an object with a single property named `profile_image`, which was the name of our image, with a number of properties. These properties contain relevant information about the uploaded files.

It is beyond the scope of this book to get into the details of all the properties, but the following are must-knows to be able to work with file uploads in Express:

Property	Description
`size`	Size of the file in kilobytes
`path`	Temporary location of the uploaded file
`name`	Name of the file as uploaded
`type`	Media type of the file

It might come as a surprise for you, but Express provides all the necessary information about the uploaded files, but it does nothing apart from giving it random names and moving it to a temporary location.

It is the developer's responsibility to actually move the uploaded files to the right location, rename if necessary, resize, and so on.

The files will be uploaded to the temporary directory of the operating system. On a Linux machine, it may look like `/tmp/4e552b0243d20a171f287a687d744b45` and so on, with no extensions. If you want to preserve the extension, set the `keepExtension` property to `true`.

```
app.use(express.bodyParser({keepExtensions: true}));
```

Uploading files to a temporary location with random names isn't really useful, so let's re-write the route to move the uploaded files to `public/uploads`.

The reason why temporary files have very random names is to prevent name collisions if files with the same names are uploaded.

Since we will need to perform filesystem actions, we will need to include the `fs` module:

```
var fs = require('fs');
```

The `fs` module deals with everything related to the filesystem in Node.js. You can read more about it at `http://nodejs.org/api/fs.html`.

Next, we will modify the route handler. Make sure to include the callback function (`next`), because we need it for handling any errors that might be encountered:

```
app.post('/signup', function(req, res, next) {

  var name = req.body.name;
  var email = req.body.email;

  // Reference to the profile_image object
  var profile_image = req.files.profile_image;

  // Temporary location of the uploaded file
  var tmp_path = profile_image.path;
  // New location of the file
  var target_path = './public/images/' + profile_image.name;
  // Move the file from the new location
  // fs.rename() will create the necessary directory
  fs.rename(tmp_path, target_path, function(err) {
      // If an error is encountered, pass it to the next handler
      if (err) { next(err); }
      // Delete the temporary file
      fs.unlink(tmp_path, function() {
        // If an error is encountered, pass it to the next handler
          if (err) { next(err); }
          console.log('File uploaded to: ' + target_path + ' - ' +
profile_image.size + ' bytes');
          res.redirect('/images/' + profile_image.name);
      });
  });

});
```

The updated route handler will print some details about the file on the console and redirect the browser to the uploaded file, if everything goes successfully.

In the preceding example, a new file with the same name as one already uploaded will overwrite the existing one. The example is just to show how to move uploaded files to a proper destination.

More about file uploads

A reference is created in the `req.files` object for each uploaded file. If you upload multiple files in a form, all of them will have a reference in this object. You can process them all by looping through the `req.files` object:

```
req.files.forEach(function(file) {
  // Code to handle the file
  ...
});
```

Although files are uploaded to the system's temporary directory, we can change the default behavior by setting the value of `uploadDir` to any location of our choice:

```
app.use(express.bodyParser({uploadDir:'./uploads'}));
```

Express won't create the upload directory for you if it does not exist already, instead, it will throw an error. So make sure you create the directory before uploading files, when you set the `uploadDir` option.

Here is the code snippet for setting the `uploadDir` option and creating the upload directory, if it does not exist already:

```
var upload_dir = './uploads';
var exists = fs.existsSync(upload_dir);
if (!exists) {
  fs.mkdirSync(upload_dir);
}

app.use(express.bodyParser({uploadDir: upload_dir}));
```

It is important to note that the files uploaded to the temporary directory would eventually be cleared by the OS, but when using a custom upload directory, it is the developer's responsibility to clear the temporary files.

Submission via simulated methods

Technically, the HTML form is capable of making GET and POST requests only. However, Express has a trick to allow HTML forms to make any kind of HTTP request with the use of the `methodOverride` middleware. This trick is commonly known as **HTTP method overriding**.

One reason why you might want to implement HTTP method overriding would be to create RESTful interfaces to your web app. You can read more about REST at `https://en.wikipedia.org/wiki/Representational_state_transfer`.

The `methodOverride` middleware lets you "convert" POST requests to any other valid HTTP method. This is done by including a POST parameter named `_method` and setting its value to the method of your choice.

If this explanation didn't make sense to you, try this:

There is an understanding between the HTML form and Express. The form tells Express, "Hey, we both know this is a POST request, but treat it like it was requested via the method specified in the `_method` parameter", and Express treats the request as such.

So there it is, we can simulate any kind of submission using the `methodOverride` middleware. This middleware is should be loaded after the `bodyParser` middleware and before the `router` middleware:

```
app.use(express.bodyParser());
app.use(express.methodOverride());
app.use(app.router);
```

Following is an example of a form that is ready to be submitted using the PUT method. Note, we are setting the `_method` parameter in a hidden form element with the value set to `put`:

```
form(action='/request', method='post')
    label Name
    input(type='text', name='name')
    input(type='hidden', name='_method', value='put')
    br
    input(type='submit')
```

And here is the route and the handler for this request:

```
app.put('/request', function(req, res) {
  console.log('PUT: ' + req.body.name);
```

```
    res.send('PUT: ' + req.body.name);
});
```

A good thing about HTTP method overriding is that all the POST request handling features continue to work as expected—even files.

We use the `_method` parameter as a flag for indicating the method with which to override. However, if you want to use the `_method` parameter for other purposes, you can create your own flag for indicating the overriding method—just pass a string to the middleware:

```
app.use(express.methodOverride('_method_'));
```

With this, Express will look for `_method_` instead of `_method` for the method with which to override the POST request.

Note that method override works only with forms submitted using the POST method.

Data in named segments

We were introduced to named segments in *Chapter 3, Understanding Express Routes*. It needs a special mention in this chapter because it is one of the most common media for sending data to the server, along with forms and cookies.

In named segments, we create routes with segments in the URL marked as placeholders for values. When such a route is accessed, the values of the placeholders are available in variables named after the placeholders. This feature enables queries to look neater by making them look like regular URLs.

Here is a URL with data contained in a query string:

```
http://localhost:3000/user?id=89
```

The preceding URL can be converted to a cleaner-looking URL using named parameters:

```
http://localhost:3000/user/89
```

Reading data

Named segment values are available in the `req.params` object after we create the appropriate routing.

The following route is defined to work with the `http://localhost:3000/user/89` URL:

```
app.get('/user/:id', function(req, res) {
  console.log('User ID: '+ req.params.id);
  res.send('User ID: '+ req.params.id);
});
```

Because dots and dashes are interpreted as literals when used with named segments, we can use this fact for interesting results.

Define the following route and load `http://localhost:3000/file/profile.jpg` in the browser:

```
// This example will fail if the file name has a dot in it
app.get('/file/:name.:ext', function(req, res) {

  var name = req.params.name;
  var ext = req.params.ext;

  console.log('File: ' + name);
  console.log('Ext: ' + ext);

  var log = 'Name: ' + name + '<br>' + 'Ext: ' + ext;
  res.send(log);

});
```

The following route uses dash to accept `to` and `from` parameters:

```
app.get('/route/:from-:to', function(req, res) {

  var from = req.params.from;
  var to = req.params.to;

  console.log('From: ' + from);
  console.log('To: ' + to);

  var log = 'From: ' + from + '<br>' + 'To: ' + to;
  res.send(log);

});
```

Load `http://localhost:3000/route/NYC-LAX` in the browser to see the route in action.

Since named segments are part of the URL, they can be used by any HTTP method.

Although named segments make for cleaner URLs, switching the position of parameters will result in erroneous results.

There is a method called `req.param()` that can read the parameter value from `req.params`, `req.body`, and `req.query`, in that order, depending on where the values are defined. It can cause confusing bugs. Avoid using it, unless absolutely required.

Using cookies to store data

Cookies are small bits of information that a website can store in a user's browser. They may be used for various purposes, from providing users with a customized and lively experience to surreptitiously tracking their browsing habits.

Cookies can be created by the server backend or the frontend JavaScript. They can then be read or updated by either one of them.

Install a cookie-editing extension such as **Edit This Cookie** in Google Chrome to interactively experiment with the cookies created in your browser.

Express provides a cookie API using the `cookieParser` middleware. To enable the cookie functionality in Express, load it before the `router` middleware:

```
app.use(express.cookieParser());
```

With this middleware enabled, you can find the cookies sent by the browser in the `req.cookies` object, and set cookies using the `res.cookie()` method.

The `cookieParser` middleware must be loaded before the `router` middleware; else cookie functionality will not be enabled.

That was a short introduction to how the Express cookie API works; let's explore the API in greater details using some examples.

Creating cookies

Cookies are created using the `res.cookie()` method. You pass it the name of the cookie, its value, and an optional object with the cookie options.

Let's create a route named `counter` and use the `res.cookie()` method to create a cookie if it is not there already, and increment its value if it exists already.

```
app.get('/counter', function(req, res) {
```

```
    var count = req.cookies.count || 0;
    count++;
    res.cookie('count', count);
    res.send('Count: ' + count);

});
```

Load `http://localhost:3000/counter` in your browser and keep refreshing it to see the cookie created and its value being incremented:

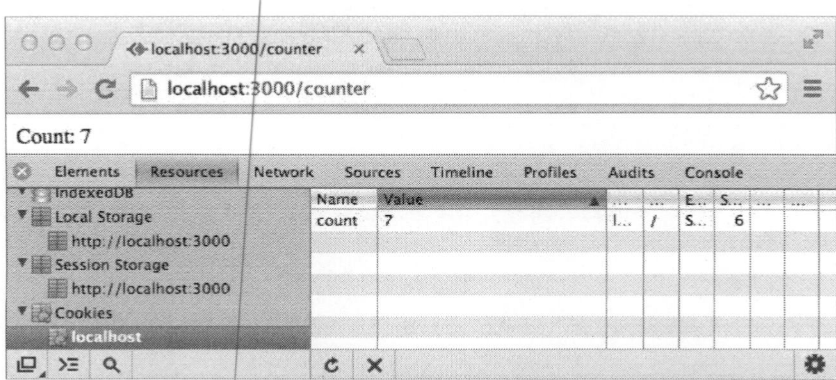

The `res.cookie()` method accepts an optional cookie options object. The following table displays a list of possible options that can be specified:

Option	Description
`domain`	Domain name for the cookie. Defaults to the domain name `loaded`.
`path`	Path for the cookie. Defaults to "/".
`secure`	Marks the cookie to be used with HTTPS only.
`expires`	Expiry date of the cookie in GMT. If not specified or set to `0`, creates a session cookie.
`maxAge`	Convenient option for setting the expiry time relative to the current time in milliseconds.
`httpOnly`	Flags the cookie to be accessible only to the web server. It helps prevent XSS attacks by disallowing client-side JavaScript access to it.
`signed`	Indicates if the cookie should be signed. Signed cookies cannot be tampered with without invalidating them.

Here is an example of setting a cookie with some options:

```
res.cookie('count', count, {
  path: '/counter',
  maxAge: 2000
});
```

Make sure to call the cookie creation method before `res.send()` or `res.render()` or other similar methods that terminate the HTTP response. Cookies are set via the HTTP header, and when we try to set a cookie after terminating the HTTP response, we will encounter an error message that says "can't set headers after they are sent".

Reading cookies

All cookies valid for the domain and path are available on the `cookies` property of the request object: `req.cookies`. For example, if you created a cookie called `count`, its value will be available on `req.cookies.count`.

Updating cookies

Updating a cookie is just about re-creating it with a new set of properties. Assuming we already created a cookie named `counter`, this is how we would update it:

```
res.cookie('counter', new_value);
```

Session cookies

Session cookies are those that last for a browsing session and are discarded after the browser is closed.

When the `expires` option is not specified, Express creates a session cookie:

```
res.cookie('name', 'Napoleon');
```

Setting the `expires` option to `0` also creates a session cookie:

```
res.cookie('name', 'Napoleon', {expires: 0});
```

If you have set your browser to remember the tabs that were open when you re-launch it, session cookies may not be deleted on closing the browser.

Signed cookies

Signed cookies are those that come with a signature attached to its value. The signature is generated using a secret string, which you can specify in the `cookieParser` middleware. When such cookies are manually tampered with, it is detected and they are invalidated.

To create a signed cookie, pass a string to the `cookieParser` middleware while instantiating it.

```
app.use(express.cookieParser('S3CRE7'));
```

Signed cookies are located in a special object called `signedCookies` on the request object. Don't make the mistake of looking for them in the `cookies` property of the request object.

Here is an example of signing and retrieving a signed cookie:

```
app.get('/counter', function(req, res) {

  var count = req.signedCookies.count || 0;
  count++;
  res.cookie('count', count, { signed: true });
  res.send('Count: ' + count);

});
```

Start the app and load `http://localhost:3000/counter` to see the signed cookie getting created, read, and updated. To test the fact that it can detect tampering, use a cookie-editing browser extension and try editing its value:

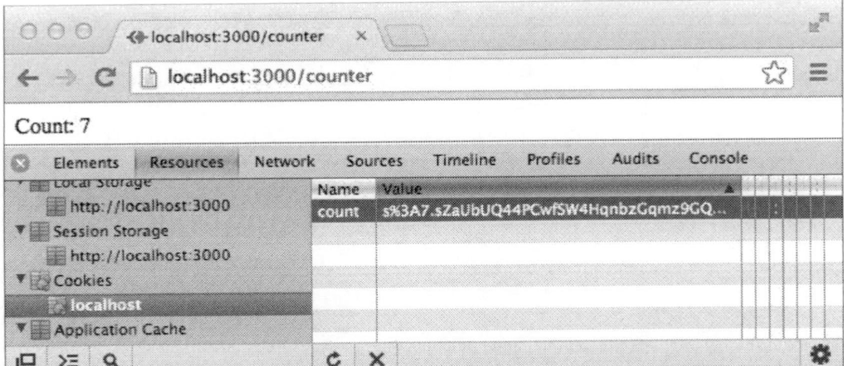

> Signed cookies are not encrypted or hidden from the user's view. They just have a signature associated with the value that can be used to ensure the cookie values are not tampered with.
>
> The secret passed to the `cookieParser` middleware is used to generate a signature for the original cookie value and the value submitted back by the browser; if the values don't match, it is understood that the value has been tampered with.

Deleting cookies

Session cookies are deleted when the browser is closed; other cookies are deleted when the expiry date is reached. However, we have complete programmatic power to delete them any time we want using the `res.clearCookie()` method.

It is important to make sure we call the `res.clearCookie()` method with the right domain name and path options, or else the cookies won't be deleted.

Here are some examples of creating cookies and the corresponding methods of deleting them:

Create	Delete
`res.cookie('count', 99);`	`res.clearCookie('count');`
`res.cookie('count', 99, {path: '/counter'});`	`res.clearCookie('count', {path: '/counter'});`
`res.cookie('count', 99, {sign: true});`	`res.clearCookie('count');`

Using sessions to store data

While we can use cookies for storing information relevant to a user, it starts to become unwieldy as their number increases and the size of the data grows. That's where sessions come in.

Sessions, however, should not be mistaken for an independent replacement for cookies. In fact, the sessions API leverages a cookie to identify a user's session.

There are two broad ways of implementing sessions in Express: using cookies and using a session store at the backend. Both of them add a new object in the request object named `session`, which contains the session variables.

No matter which method you use, Express provides a consistent interface for interacting with the session data.

Cookie-based sessions

Using the fact that cookies can store data in the user's browser, a session API can be implemented using cookies. Express comes with a built-in middleware called `cookieSession` that does just that.

Load the `cookieParser` middleware with a secret, followed by the `cookieSession` middleware, before the `router` middleware. The `cookieSession` middleware is dependent on the `cookieParser` middleware because it uses a cookie for storing the session data.

The `cookieParser` middleware should be initialized with a secret, because `cookieSession` needs to generate a signed `HttpOnly` cookie for storing the session data. If you don't specify a secret for `cookieParser`, you will need to specify the secret option of `cookieSsession`.

The following is a code for enabling sessions in Express using the `cookieSession` middleware:

```
app.use(express.cookieParser('S3CRE7'));
app.use(express.cookieSession());
app.use(app.router);
```

Although the `cookieSession` middleware can be initialized without any options, the middleware accepts an options object with the following possible options:

Option	Description
`key`	Name of the cookie. Defaults to `connect.sess`.
`secret`	Secret for signing the session. Required if `cookieParser` is not initialized with one.
`cookie`	Session cookie settings. Regular cookie defaults apply.
`proxy`	To trust the reverse proxy or not. Defaults to `false`.

Here is an example of initializing `cookieSession` with some options:

```
app.use(express.cookieSession({
  key: 'app.sess',
  secret: 'SUPERsekret'
}));
```

Once the session API is enabled, session variables can be accessed on the session object on the request object: `req.session`.

> Working with `req.session` is like working with any other JavaScript object. For more details, you can skip to the *Session Variables* section in this chapter.

Cookie-based sessions work great for simple session data. However, it doesn't work well with large, complicated, and sensitive data because the session data is visible to the user. There is a limit on the size of cookies a browser can store, and multiple large size cookies can affect the performance of the website.

The limitations in cookie-based sessions can be overcome by sessions based on session stores.

Session store-based sessions

A session store is a provision for storing session data in the backend. Sessions based on session stores can store a large amount of data that is well hidden from the user.

The `session` middleware provides a way of creating sessions using session stores. Like `cookieSession`, the `session` middleware is dependent on the `cookieParser` middleware for creating a signed `HttpOnly` cookie.

Initializing the `session` middleware is a lot like initializing `cookieSession`—we first load `cookieParser` with a secret, and load the `session` middleware before the `router` middleware:

```
app.use(express.cookieParser('S3CRE7'));
app.use(express.session());
app.use(app.router);
```

The `session` middleware accepts an options object that can be used for defining the options of the middleware. The following are the supported options:

Option	Description
`key`	Name of the cookie. Defaults to `connect.sid`.
`store`	Instance of a session store. Defaults to `MemoryStore`. The session store may support options of its own.
`secret`	Secret for signing session cookie. Required if not passed to `cookieParser()`.
`cookie`	Session cookie settings. Regular cookie defaults apply.
`proxy`	To trust the reverse proxy or not. Defaults to `false`.

Here is an example of initializing the `session` middleware with some options:

```
app.use(express.session({
  key: 'app.sess',
  store: new RedisStore,
  secret: 'SEKR37'
}));
```

It is beyond the scope of this book but it is worth mentioning that you can write your own session store if you want.

Express defines an interface for creating session stores, as long as you adhere to the specifications, you can create your own session store using any database or data-storage mechanism.

The interface for accessing and working with the session variables remain the same: `req.session`, except now the session values reside on the backend.

Let's explore three popular session stores for Express.

MemoryStore

Express comes with a built-in session store called `MemoryStore`, which is the default when you don't specify one explicitly.

`MemoryStore` uses the application RAM for storing session data and works right out of the box, without the need for any database. Seeing how easily it is to set up, you might be tempted to make it the session store of your choice, but it is not recommended to do so because of the following reasons:

- Memory consumption will keep growing with each new session
- In case the app is restarted for any reason, all session data will be lost
- Session data cannot be shared by other instances of the app in a cluster

In fact, if you try to use `MemoryStore` in a production environment, you will get the following warning:

```
Warning: connection.session() MemoryStore is not
designed for a production environment, as it will leak
memory, and will not scale past a single process.
```

Although `MemoryStore` is not a scalable solution and is not recommended on production, it makes for a good choice for getting to know the session API quickly and developing the application without the need for any database.

RedisStore

`RedisStore` is a popular third-party module that uses Redis for storing session data.

Redis is a popular key-value "database" that is known for its speed in storing and retrieving data. To learn more about Redis, visit `http://redis.io/`.

Since `RedisStore` uses Redis for storing session data, you will need to have an instance of Redis running locally or on a remote server.

Install `RedisStore` in the application directory:

```
$ npm install connect-redis
```

Load the `RedisStore` module in the app and pass the instance of the Express object to it:

```
var express = require('express');
var RedisStore = require('connect-redis')(express);
```

With that, we are ready to use `RedisStore` as our session store—load the `session` middleware with its `store` option set to an instance of `RedisStore`:

```
app.use(express.session({ store: new RedisStore }));
```

`RedisStore` accepts a configuration object that can be used for specifying various aspects of the session store:

```
app.use(express.session({ store: new RedisStore({
  host:'127.0.0.1',
  port:6380,
  prefix:'sess'
}), secret: 'SEKR37' }));
```

Once you have set up `RedisStore` successfully, you can continue to work on the `req.session` object to create, read, update, and delete session variables as usual; only this time, the data is stored on a Redis server, accessible by multiple instances of your app and persisting if your app is restarted.

You can get more information about `RedisStore` at `https://github.com/visionmedia/connect-redis`.

MongoStore

Another popular session store uses MongoDB for storing the data and is called `MongoStore`. The usage pattern is very similar to `RedisStore`.

MongoDB is a very popular NoSQL database that uses a binary version of JSON, BSON, to store data. Known for its speed and easy of use, it is a popular choice of database for many modern web projects.

For MongoStore to work with your app, you will need to have an instance of MongoDB running on your local system or on a remote server.

You can learn more about MongoDB at `http://www.mongodb.org/`.

Install `MongoStore` in the application directory:

```
$ npm install connect-mongo
```

Load the `MongoStore` module in the app and set an instance of it as the session store for the `session` middleware:

```
var express = require('express');
var MongoStore = require('connect-mongo')(express);
...
app.use(express.session({
  store: new MongoStore({
    db: 'myapp',
    host: '127.0.0.1',
    port: 3355
  })
}));
```

With that, session data will now be stored in MongoDB, but the session interface remains the same—the `req.session` object.

You can read more about MongoStore at `https://github.com/kcbanner/connect-mongo`.

Session variables

Session variables are those variables that you associate with a user session. These variables are independently set for each user and can be accessed on the `session` property of the request object (`req.session`).

While it might look like we are dealing with a JavaScript object, it is not completely true; the session variables actually reside in the data store of the session and the JavaScript object only works as a proxy for those values.

Operations on session variables are basically working with JavaScript objects. The states of these objects are then updated on the session store.

Setting session variables

To set a session variable, attach it to the `req.session` object:

```
req.session.name = 'Napoleon';
```

In case the session variable contains illegal characters, use a substring notation to create it:

```
req.session['primary skill'] = 'Dancing';
```

Reading session variables

Session variables can be read from the `res.session` object using either the dot notation or the substring notation:

```
var name = req.session.name;
var primary_skill = req.session['primary skill'];
```

If you try to read an undefined property, you will get undefined as expected.

Updating session variables

Updating a session variable is just about updating the property in the `req.session` object or overwriting the existing property with a new value:

```
// Assuming req.session.skills and req.session.name were already
defined
req.session.skills.push('Baking');
req.session.name = 'Pedro';
```

Deleting session variables

To delete a session variable, just delete the property from the `req.session` object:

```
delete req.session.name
delete req.session['primary skill'];
```

> If you are wondering whether `req.session.skills = null;` would work, the value will persist in the session as `null`, not be really deleted. Remember we are dealing with session data, not JavaScript variables.

Deleting a session

We learned that there are two broad ways of creating sessions: using `cookieSession` and `sessionStore`. Each session type has its own way of deleting the session.

Deleting a cookie-based session

To delete a cookie-based session, just delete the `session` object from the request object, or set it to `null`:

```
deletereq.session;
```

or

```
req.session = null;
```

Once the `session` object is deleted, the session cookie is also deleted from the browser, effectively destroying the session.

Deleting a session store-based session

Session store-based sessions do not interpret a missing `session` object on the request object as the end of a session. If we delete the `session` object from the request object, it will be recreated from the session store, because the session store decides the state of the session, not JavaScript variables. This also the reason why these sessions are intact even after the app restarts.

Session store-based sessions have a method called `destroy()` that is used for destroying sessions from the session store—the proper way of tearing down a session store-based session:

```
req.session.destroy();
```

The `destroy()` method accepts an optional callback function to be executed after the session is cleared from the store:

```
req.session.destroy(function() {
  res.send('Session deleted');
});
```

For the curious ones, `cookieSession` does not have a `destroy()` method; trying to call the `destroy()` method on a session created using `cookieSession` will throw an error.

Summary

In this chapter, we learned how to submit forms using various HTTP methods, learned how to create cookies and understood how to implement sessions in Express using various ways.

Now that we have covered almost everything about Express, it is time to learn about the things we need to make our Express app production-ready.

8

Express in Production

So far we have been learning about and implementing various aspects of Express in sample apps on our local machine, and by now we know quite a lot about Express. However, our ultimate goal of learning Express is to be able to deploy apps on production.

This chapter is about making our app production-ready. We will learn the following in this chapter:

- How to benchmark our app
- How to make our app scale and perform well
- How to ensure maximum uptime for the app

What the is production environment?

The system on which we develop our app is the development environment or platform—the system could be your personal laptop or desktop. Apart from development, we may use such a system for browsing, sending e-mails, image editing, playing games, listening to music, watching movies, and so on. We would not host our app on such a system, would we?

When we are ready to share our app with the world, the recommended and common practice is to use a dedicated system for hosting it, which may or may not be shared by other apps.

So how does Express know it is in the production environment?

Express looks up the `NODE_ENV` environment variable to determine the environment it is in. If the environment variable is not defined, it assumes it as a development environment.

For more information about `NODE_ENV` and the various modes of Express, refer to the *Express in different environments* section in *Chapter 2, Your First Express App*.

What changes in production mode?

When Express detects that it is running in production mode, it makes the following changes automatically:

- Jade view templates are cached in memory
- CSS files are cached in the filesystem, and re-rendered only if the source Stylus file is modified
- `MemoryStore` emits a warning and will definitely not scale beyond a single process
- Error messages are less verbose

Also, we might use different configurations for development and production. We might use an app configuration file with content like this:

```
{
  development: {
    db_host: 'locahost',
    db_user: 'dev',
    db_padd: 'passm3'
  },

  production: {
    db_host: '192.168.10.12',
    db_user: 'dbuser1',
    db_padd: '0lulwu7'
  }
}
```

Refer to the *Using a configuration file* section in *Chapter 2, Your First Express App*, for details about using an application configuration file.

Simulating production environment

There will be times when we want to see how a certain aspect of our app will behave in the production environment, while still being in the development environment.

Since Express depends on the `NODE_ENV` environment variable to determine the environment, it is pretty easy to make Express behave like it is in the production environment. Just start the app with `NODE_ENV` temporarily set to `production`:

```
$ NODE_ENV=production node app
```

All production-specific changes will kick in once the environment variable is set to `production`.

Benchmarking the app

Performance is one of the primary concerns when it comes to making an app production-ready. Since a major section of this chapter is about making our app performant, it makes sense to know right at the beginning how to quantitatively measure the performance of our app.

We will use a command-line tool called **siege** for benchmarking our app. While it is not going to be the most scientific and accurate method, benchmarking with `siege` will give us a fair idea about how well our app is performing.

Here is how to install `siege` in Ubuntu:

```
$ sudo apt-get install siege
```

To start benchmarking an app located at `http://localhost:3000/`, we would benchmark it this way:

```
$ siege -b -c100 -t10S http://localhost:3000/
```

Basically, we are performing a tiny denial of service (DoS) attack on our server and seeing how well it fares.

The options used in the command are listed as follows:

Option	Description
`-b`	To indicate we are benchmarking the app. No delays between requests.
`-c`	Concurrent connections. We decided on `100`.
`-t`	Duration of benchmark. You can specify in `S` (seconds), `M` (minutes), or `H` (hours). We chose `10` seconds.

`siege` is a very versatile tool and comes with more than a dozen options. Type `siege --help` at the command line to see all the options. Explore the various options and play around with the values to match your requirements.

A benchmark result may look something like this:

```
Transactions:              188 hits
Availability:           100.00 %
Elapsed time:             9.76 secs
Data transferred:       105.58 MB
Response time:            0.80 secs
Transaction rate:        19.26 trans/sec
Throughput:           10.82 MB/sec
Concurrency:            15.44
Successful transactions:        188
Failed transactions:              0
Longest transaction:           1.96
Shortest transaction:          0.03
```

Here is a brief description of the various fields of the benchmark:

Field	Description
`Transactions`	The number of requests made.
`Availability`	The percentage of socket connections successfully handled by the server.
`Elapsed time`	The duration of the entire siege test.
`Data transferred`	The sum of data transferred to every siege-simulated user. It includes the header information as well as the content. Because it includes header information, the number reported by siege will be larger then the number reported by the server. In `internet` mode, which hits random URLs in a configuration file, this number is expected to vary from run to run.
`Response time`	The average time taken to respond to each simulated user's requests.
`Transaction rate`	The average number of transactions the server was able to handle per second.
`Throughput`	The average number of bytes transferred every second from the server to all the simulated users.

Field	Description
`Concurrency`	The average number of simultaneous connections, a number that rises as server performance decreases.
`Successful transactions`	The number of times the server returned a code less then 400.
`Failed transactions`	The number of times the server responded with a return code more than or equal to 400 plus the sum of all failed socket transactions, which includes socket timeouts.
`Longest transaction`	The longest period of time that any single transaction took, out of all transactions.
`Shortest transaction`	The least period of time that any single transaction took, out of all transactions.

To increase the reliability of the benchmark, run the app and the siege test on different machines in the network and ensure a minimum number of processes are running on them.

Benchmarking and load testing is a vast topic of its own, and out of scope of this book. As a web developer, it is recommended to learn about them.

Now that we know how to benchmark, make sure to benchmark the app after learning about each optimization technique covered in the chapter.

Creating an app cluster

One common argument against Node is that it is single-threaded and therefore does not perform well.

This argument is outdated and invalid—now Node comes with a module called `cluster`, using which we can run multiple processes of an app, essentially multiplying the performance of the app on multi-core machines, which most modern computers are.

The performance gain is more obvious when the app is processor- and memory-hungry, and is data-intensive. "Hello World" apps are likely to show little to no improvement in less stressful tests.

The `cluster` module is still experimental, so the API may change in the future. But the module itself is likely to be there for good.

Let's write two sample apps to find out whether the performance gain by using cluster is true or not. We will make sure these apps perform the same set of resource-intensive operations.

Here is the first app, a very basic Express app that programmatically generates a huge amount of data and sends it to the client:

```
var http = require('http');
var express = require('express');
var app = express();

app.get('/', function (req, res) {

  // A resource-intensive operation
  var a = [];
  for (var i = 0; i < 100000; i++) { a.push(i); }

  // A large chunk of data
  res.send(a.toString());
});

http.createServer(app).listen(3000, function() {
  console.log('Express app started');
});
```

Following is the re-write of the previous app, using `cluster`:

```
var cluster = require('cluster');

// Master process - starts the workers
if (cluster.isMaster) {

  var cpu_count = require('os').cpus().length;

  // Create a worker process for each core
  require('os').cpus().forEach(function() {

    // Start a worker process
    cluster.fork();
```

```
    });

    // In case a worker dies, a new one should be started
    cluster.on('exit', function (worker, code, signal) {
      cluster.fork();
    });

  }
  // Code for the worker processes to execute
  else {

    var worker_id = 'Worker' + cluster.worker.id;

    var http = require('http');
    var express = require('express');
    var app = express();

    app.get('/', function (req, res) {

      // An resource-intensive operation
      var a = [];
      for (var i = 0; i < 100000; i++) { a.push(i); }

      // A large chunk of data
      res.send(a.toString());
    });

    // Start the app
    http.createServer(app).listen(3000, function() {
      console.log('Express app started by %s', worker_id);
    });

  }
```

When you run this app, the code within the `if (cluster.isMaster)` bock will be executed, which will fork the worker processes. The workers will execute the code within the corresponding `else` block thereby creating their instances of the app, which is made evident from the console message.

You must have noted that we forked a process for each core in the CPU. This is because we want each core to run a single process only. There is no technical restriction on the number of workers we can fork, but running more than one process in a core does not add to the performance of the app.

Requests made to the server will now be distributed among the worker processes, which can be processed simultaneously, thus increasing the overall performance of the app.

Here is a comparative analysis of the two versions of the app benchmarked using siege for 10 seconds with 100 concurrent connections, on a quad-core laptop:

Single-process app		**Clustered app**	
`Transactions:`	`203 hits`	`Transactions:`	`498 hits`
`Availability:`	`100.00 %`	`Availability:`	`100.00 %`
`Elapsed time:`	`9.15 secs`	`Elapsed time:`	`9.69 secs`
`Data transferred:`	`114.01 MB`	`Data transferred:`	`279.68 MB`
`Response time:`	`3.87 secs`	`Response time:`	`1.23 secs`
`Transaction rate:`	`22.19 trans/sec`	`Transaction rate:`	`51.39 trans/sec`
`Throughput:`	`12.46 MB/sec`	`Throughput:`	`28.86 MB/sec`
`Concurrency:`	`85.80`	`Concurrency:`	`73.10`
`Successful transactions:`	`203`	`Successful transactions:`	`498`
`Failed transactions:`	`0`	`Failed transactions:`	`0`
`Longest transaction:`	`4.09`	`Longest transaction:`	`4.13`
`Shortest transaction:`	`0.44`	`Shortest transaction:`	`0.05`

The accuracy of benchmarking any software system depends on taking into consideration all the components and factors affecting its performance, which is a very complex and elaborate process, and beyond the affordability of individual developers and small companies.

Benchmarking an Express app on a local network on a machine with siege, while not giving the absolute truth about the performance, gives an overall good idea about the performance of the app.

You can very well see that using all the available CPU cores has greatly increased the performance of the app in most aspects.

Apart from adding to the performance of the app, using `cluster` ensures greater uptime for Node apps—if a process goes down, the remaining processes continue to handle the requests, while a new process is being forked to replace the process that exited.

It is important to note that workers do not share the same memory space; a variable defined in a worker will not be accessible to other workers. This is one of the reasons why `MemoryStore` is not recommended as the session store in production.

There is more to the `cluster` module than what was shown in the example. To be able to make the best use it, you will need to know the API as well as possible. You can read more about `cluster` at `http://nodejs.org/api/cluster.html`.

Handling critical events

All apps are susceptible to crashes and signal terminations. Production-ready apps are supposed to handle these critical events as gracefully and usefully as possible when they can, rather than crash abruptly.

In this section, we will learn how to handle fatal errors and termination signals from our app.

Closing the server

One of the first things to do in the event of something critical is to close the server to new connections, so that we can perform the necessary housekeeping before finally terminating the process.

When we start the server using `http.createServer()`, the method returns an instance of Node's web server object, which has a method called `close()` that will stop the server from receiving new requests.

You can read more about the HTTP Server object at `http://nodejs.org/docs/latest/api/http.html#http_http_createserver_requestlistener`.

Following is a simple example of using the server's `close()` method. This app will respond to the first request it receives and close the server to any new connections.

In modern browsers, a refresh or a new tab does not always mean a new connection because of HTTP persistent connection; so don't be shocked if you can still access the app from the same browser. However, the app will no longer be accessible from a different browser.

```
var http = require('http');
var express = require('express');
var app = express();
```

```
// Variable to track the status of the server
var closed = false;

app.get('/', function (req, res) {

  // First request to the server
  if (!closed) {

    // Close the server - no more new connections
    server.close();

    // Respond to the request
    res.send('First request');

    closed = true;
  }
  // Message for Kept alive connections
  else {
    res.send('Server shutting down ...');
  }

  // Shutdown the server in 5 secs
  setTimeout(function() {
    process.exit();
  }, 5000);

});

// Get the instance of the web server object
var server = http.createServer(app).listen(3000, function() {
  console.log('Express app started');
});
```

Now that we know how to close the server, let's find out how `server.close()` can be used to gracefully handle fatal errors and termination signals.

Handling uncaught errors

A bad news about Node is that uncaught errors will crash the HTTP server. The good news is that this is easily mitigated using proper error-handling techniques, clusters, and load balancing.

By default, when a runtime error occurs in an Express app, it will either be caught by the error handler defined in the `router` middleware or it will bring down the server.

Here is an example of the first kind:

```
var http = require('http');
var express = require('express');
var app = express();

app.get('/', function (req, res) {

  // Error will be caught
  get_data();

});

var server = http.createServer(app).listen(3000, function() {
  console.log('Express app started');
});
```

When you load `http://localhost:3000/`, you will get **500 Internal Server Error**, but the server is still up and running, and users can still access the functional parts of the app.

And here is an example of an uncaught error, which bubbles up to the event loop and brings down the server (we will just redefine the route from the previous app, for the sake of brevity).

```
app.get('/', function (req, res) {

  // An async operation which causes an error
  process.nextTick(function() {
    get_data();
  });

});
```

`process.nextTick()` is a low-level construct to execute instructions after the current set of instructions have been processed, making all the expressions within it asynchronous relative to the current set. You can read more about `process.nextTick()` at `http://nodejs.org/api/process.html#process_process_nexttick_callback`.

This time, when you load `http://localhost:3000/`, the app will crash instantly. So how do we handle such errors?

Using try-catch to catch uncaught errors

The first thing that comes to the mind about handling uncaught errors is to use the `try-catch` construct on operations that are likely to throw a data error.

Here is an example to handle the previous case:

```
process.nextTick(function() {
  try {
    get_data();
  }
  catch(err) {
    console.log(err);
    res.send(500, 'Oops!');
  }
});
```

Using `try-catch` can technically solve the uncaught error problem, but becomes unrealistic in complex situations. Following is an example to demonstrate this fact:

```
process.nextTick(function() {
  try {
    process.nextTick(function() {
      set_data();
    });
    get_data();
  }
  catch(err) {
    console.log(err);
    res.send(500, 'Oops!');
  }
});
```

In Node, any async function can contain a potential app-crashing operation. How deep do we use `try-catch`, and how many can we use? It starts to become impractical beyond a certain limit.

> Node provides an event named `uncaughtException` in the `process` object, listening to which can catch process-level uncaught errors. When this event is listened for, the default behavior of terminating the process on uncaught errors is prevented. However, it is officially recognized as inefficient and is likely to be removed in the future versions of Node, so don't count on it.

Using domains to handle uncaught errors

A new Node module called `domain` was introduced in Node 0.8.0 for handling errors more efficiently. A `domain` is like a flexible error handler for any and all errors that might be thrown within it. Unlike `uncaughtException`, `domain` maintains the context of the objects that were involved in the exception. Using domains is the recommended method for handling uncaught errors in Node.

The `domain` module is currently marked as Unstable, meaning, the API may change in the future. So make it a point to keep yourself updated with the changes.

Here is a very simple example for catching an unhandled error using the `domain` module:

```
var http = require('http');
var express = require('express');
var app = express();
var domain = require('domain');

app.get('/', function (req, res) {

  // Instantiate a domain
  var d = domain.create();

  // Domain error handler
  d.on('error', function(err) {
    // Error stack
    console.log(err.stack);
    // Other information
    console.log(req.ip);
    // We still have the object in context
    res.send(500, 'Oops!');
  });

  // Execute the code under this to catch unhandled errors from it
  d.run(function() {

    // An async operation which will cause a process-level error
    process.nextTick(function() {
      get_data();
    });
  });
```

```
});

var server = http.createServer(app).listen(3000, function() {
  console.log('Express app started');
});
```

In this example, the source of the error is known to us therefore we can continue running the server. However, in production apps, an unhandled error is usually unexpected and associated with an unreliable state of the system, so it is best to gracefully shutdown the server.

Assuming we will be deploying a clustered app, here is a simple example of a `domain` error handler from a worker.

```
// Domain error handler
d.on('error', function(err) {

  // Stop accepting new connections
  server.close();

  // Perform last-minute cleanup
  res.send(500);

  // Let the master know the worker has disconnected
  cluster.worker.disconnect();

  // Terminate the process in 5 seconds
  setTimeout(function() {
    // Exit with a failure code
    process.process.exit(1);
  }, 5000);

});
```

Correspondingly, the master process should be listening to the `disconnect` event of its workers and forking a new worker accordingly:

```
// A worker reports its disconnection
cluster.on('disconnect', function(worker) {
  // For a new worker
  cluster.fork();
});
```

In our example, we covered only the `run()` method, the `domain` module supports many more methods for efficiently handling errors generated within it. You can read more about domains at `http://nodejs.org/api/domain.html`.

What to do in case of uncaught errors – to terminate the process or not to terminate?

As mentioned earlier, an uncaught error is a symptom of something seriously wrong in the app. When such an error occurs, it becomes hard to rely on the state of the app, and the default behavior of Node is to terminate the process.

From the official Node documentation:

> *"By the very nature of how throw works in JavaScript, there is almost never any way to safely "pick up where you left off", without leaking references, or creating some other sort of undefined brittle state."*

The recommended strategy for handling uncaught errors is to shut down the server gracefully. First close the server, respond to the current requests, log the event, terminate the process, and then fork a new worker.

As a developer, then you would need to find out what is causing the uncaught error and fix it at the source.

Make sure to listen for the `error` event on all instances of objects inheriting from the `EventEmitter`, and know that all async operations, such as callback functions and timers can contain code that can potentially cause uncaught errors.

Handling process termination

Our Express app may be terminated using various termination signals. Instead of letting them shut down the process abruptly, we should perform the necessary housekeeping and finally terminate the process ourselves from our code.

Here is an example for handling the two most, termination signals: `SIGINT` and `SIGTERM`:

```
// Default kill signal
process.on('SIGTERM', function() {
  // Close the server
  server.close();
  // Log the event
  console.log('Terminated at ' + Date.now());
  process.exit();
});

// CTRL+c
process.on('SIGINT', function() {
```

```
        // Close the server
        server.close();
        // Log event
        console.log('Terminated from console at ' + Date.now());
        process.exit();
    });
```

Our app can listen for all valid termination signals, except `SIGKILL`, you can read more about termination signals at `http://www.gnu.org/software/libc/manual/html_node/Termination-Signals.html`. Attempting to listen for `SIGKILL` will throw an error.

Note that the act of listening for termination signals prevents the default behavior of terminating the process when they are received, therefore, we have to programmatically terminate it after we are done with the housekeeping by using the `process.exit()` method.

Unlike unhandled errors, it may not be a good idea to fork a new process on receiving a termination signal.

Ensuring uptime

We have seen that if a worker process crashes, a new one can be forked by the master process, while the remaining workers can handle the current requests. But what happens when the master process itself crashes?

Uptime concerns are a unique aspect of Node apps, but with proper knowledge and the right tools this concern can be addressed to satisfaction.

Let's look at two popular tools for ensuring Express apps are up and running, with as little downtime as possible.

Forever

Ensuring a Node app is restarted when it goes down can easily be accomplished with the help of a Node package called `forever`.

Install `forever` as global module, so that we can use it as a command-line tool:

```
$ npm install forever -g
```

After `forever` is installed, type `forever --help` at the command line to see the various options and commands.

Here is a list of the most common commands to help you get started:

Command	Description
`$ forever start app.js`	Starts `app.js` in the background and restarts it if it crashes.
`$ forever list`	Lists all the processes started by `forever`.
`$ forever stop <process index>`	Stops the process with the specific index. Index value is retrieved from the `list` command.
`$ forever restart <process index>`	Restarts the process with the specific index. Index value is retrieved from the `list` command.

Forever does a good job of keeping a process running and restarting it if it crashes. However, it has a drawback: when the system reboots, we will have to manually restart all of the `forever` processes all over again.

Although rebooting might be an infrequent event, it doesn't sound very efficient, does it? Is there a way to automate restarting the processes?

Upstart

Upstart is a tool for starting services on Linux machines. Although it can be used for many purposes in many different ways, we will focus on how to use it for starting our app when the system starts and restarting if it crashes.

On a shared hosting environment, you might be limited to the access and functionality of `upstart`. In such cases, you will have to make do with `forever`, with a clever combination of a `cron` job.

Upstart jobs reside as `.conf` files in the `/etc/init` directory on Ubuntu. The name of the job is derived from the name of the file. For example, if the file is named `myapp.conf`, the job would be `myapp`.

Upstart jobs then can be stopped, started, and restarted from the command line in the following manner:

Command	Functionality
`start myapp`	To start the `myapp` job
`restart myapp`	To restart the `myapp` job
`stop myapp`	To stop the `myapp` job

Following is an example `upstart` job to start an Express app on system startup and ensure it is restarted when it goes down. Save it as `myapp.conf` under `/etc/init`:

```
description "Daemonized Express App"
author "Hack Sparrow"

# When to start the process
start on runlevel [2345]
# When to stop the process
stop on runlevel [016]

# The process to start
exec sudo -u www-data /usr/local/bin/node /home/captain/projects/
example/app.js

# Restart the process if it is down
respawn
# Limit restart attempt to 10 times within 10 seconds
respawn limit 10 10
```

It is beyond the scope of this book to cover everything about `upstart`, but the example should get you started with it. You can read more about `upstart` at `http://upstart.ubuntu.com/`.

If you have a dedicated server with root access on production, `upstart` is the recommended way to ensure the uptime of your Express app.

Using a reverse proxy

Express is capable of performing everything that is expected of a modern web server, such as logging requests, HTTPS, serving files and so on, but it is best used as an application server behind a reverse proxy. That way, Express can focus solely on processing dynamic requests, while other tasks can be offloaded to the reverse proxy, thereby increasing the performance of the app.

It is a standard practice in the industry to put a front-facing proxy (another name for reverse proxy) in front of a series of application servers to load-balance and scale the app.

The following illustration shows how an application server works with a reverse proxy to serve a website. In a load-balanced setup, there would be more upstream application servers:

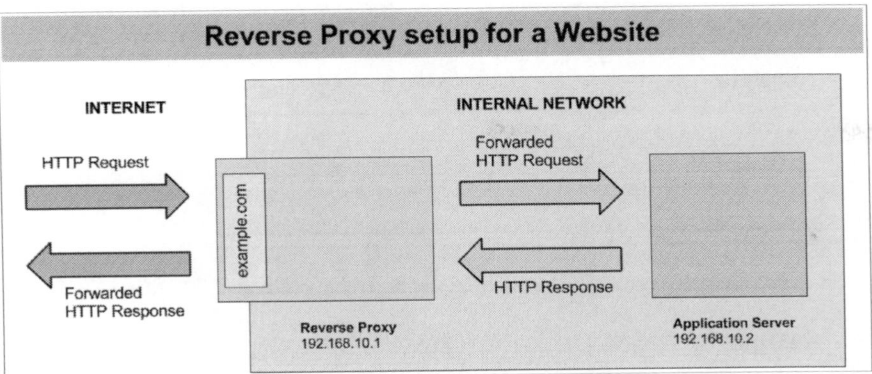

Here are some of the tasks that can be performed by Express, but are best handled by the reverse proxy:

Task	Description
Logging requests and errors	Keeping track of requests made to the server and HTTP errors generated.
Serving static files	Serving static files such as CSS, JavaScript, images, and other downloadables.
Caching	Serving current copies of files instead of regenerating them from the source.
gzip compression	Serving a compressed version of text files, thereby decreasing the load time.
HTTPS	HTTP over SSL.
Protection from malformed requests	Detects and invalidate potentially malicious protocol-level requests.

You can evaluate **nginx** (`http://nginx.org/`) and **HAProxy** (`http://haproxy.1wt.eu/`) as the potential choice of reverse proxy for your app.

The trust proxy option

Once our app is set up to run behind a reverse proxy, we should set the `trust proxy` application setting to `true`:

```
app.set('trust proxy', true);
```

On not doing so, `req.ip` will read the IP address of the proxy as the IP address of the client, which would obviously be wrong. Besides, we will be able to get the series of proxies the client has connected through from the `req.ips` property.

In case the proxy does not provide the `x-forwarded-for` header, `req.ip` will return the proxy's IP address.

Summary

In this chapter, we learned how to benchmark our app using siege. We saw that clustering increases the performance of the app in general. And then we learned how to handle fatal errors and ensure maximum uptime for our app.

Although we covered some crucial aspects of making our app production-ready, running an app on production is a vast and continuous process. Take this chapter as the starting point and learn more about the details of scaling and enhancing your app on production.

Index

Symbols

A

E

F

G

H

I

J

Q

R

S

T

U

V

W

Thank you for buying

Express Web Application Development

About Packt Publishing

Packt, pronounced 'packed', published its first book "*Mastering phpMyAdmin for Effective MySQL Management*" in April 2004 and subsequently continued to specialize in publishing highly focused books on specific technologies and solutions.

Our books and publications share the experiences of your fellow IT professionals in adapting and customizing today's systems, applications, and frameworks. Our solution based books give you the knowledge and power to customize the software and technologies you're using to get the job done. Packt books are more specific and less general than the IT books you have seen in the past. Our unique business model allows us to bring you more focused information, giving you more of what you need to know, and less of what you don't.

Packt is a modern, yet unique publishing company, which focuses on producing quality, cutting-edge books for communities of developers, administrators, and newbies alike. For more information, please visit our website: `www.packtpub.com`.

About Packt Open Source

In 2010, Packt launched two new brands, Packt Open Source and Packt Enterprise, in order to continue its focus on specialization. This book is part of the Packt Open Source brand, home to books published on software built around Open Source licences, and offering information to anybody from advanced developers to budding web designers. The Open Source brand also runs Packt's Open Source Royalty Scheme, by which Packt gives a royalty to each Open Source project about whose software a book is sold.

Writing for Packt

We welcome all inquiries from people who are interested in authoring. Book proposals should be sent to author@packtpub.com. If your book idea is still at an early stage and you would like to discuss it first before writing a formal book proposal, contact us; one of our commissioning editors will get in touch with you.

We're not just looking for published authors; if you have strong technical skills but no writing experience, our experienced editors can help you develop a writing career, or simply get some additional reward for your expertise.

Instant Node.js Starter

ISBN: 978-1-78216-556-9 Paperback: 48 pages

Program your scalable network applications and web services with Node.js

1. Learn something new in an Instant! A short, fast, focused guide delivering immediate results
2. Learn how to use module patterns and Node Packet Manager (NPM) in your applications
3. Discover callback patterns in NodeJS
4. Understand the use Node.js streams in your applications

CoffeeScript Programming with jQuery, Rails, and Node.js

ISBN: 978-1-84951-958-8 Paperback: 140 pages

Learn CoffeeScript programming with the three most popular web technologies around

1. Learn CoffeeScript, a small and elegant language that compiles to JavaScript and will make your life as a web developer better
2. Explore the syntax of the language and see how it improves and enhances JavaScript
3. Build three example applications in CoffeeScript step by step

Please check **www.PacktPub.com** for information on our titles

Made in the USA
Lexington, KY
25 November 2013